THE JUDAICA IMPRINT
FOR THOUGHTFUL PEOPLE

Seize the

RABBI ABRAHAM J. TWERSKI, M.D.
Moments

Captivating Nuggets of Torah Wisdom

© Copyright 2011 by Shaar Press

First edition – First impression / May 2011

ALL RIGHTS RESERVED
No part of this book may be reproduced **in any form,** *photocopy, electronic media, or otherwise without* **written** *permission from the copyright holder, except by a reviewer who wishes to quote brief passages in connection with a review written for inclusion in magazines or newspapers.*
THE RIGHTS OF THE COPYRIGHT HOLDER WILL BE STRICTLY ENFORCED.

Published by **SHAAR PRESS**
Distributed by MESORAH PUBLICATIONS, LTD.
4401 Second Avenue / Brooklyn, N.Y 11232 / (718) 921-9000

Distributed in Israel by SIFRIATI / A. GITLER
6 Hayarkon Street / Bnei Brak 51127

Distributed in Europe by LEHMANNS
Unit E, Viking Business Park, Rolling Mill Road / Jarrow, Tyne and Wear, NE32 3DP/ England

Distributed in Australia and New Zealand by GOLDS WORLD OF JUDAICA
3-13 William Street / Balaclava, Melbourne 3183 / Victoria Australia

Distributed in South Africa by KOLLEL BOOKSHOP
Ivy Common / 105 William Road / Norwood 2192, Johannesburg, South Africa

ISBN 10: 1-4226-1095-0 / ISBN 13: 978-1-4226-1095-4

Custom bound by Sefercraft, Inc. / 4401 Second Avenue / Brooklyn N.Y. 11232

Table of Contents

Introduction 9
Living According to Halachah 11
The Risk of Personal Interest 14
Unsuspected Theft 16
Mandated Love 18
Developing Emotions (I) 20
Developing Emotions (II) 22
The Power of the Word 25
Permissible Revenge 27
Modeling Addiction 29
The Primacy of Middos 31
The Miracle of the Human Body 33
The Chesed of Yielding 35
Tu B'Av — The Greatest of Our Holidays 37
Guilt vs. Shame 40
Kosher Money 42
Truth and Humility 44
Praise of Gratitude 46
A Loud but Silent Cry 48
Beware of Offended Pride 50
Too Good to Be Good 52
When Have I Done Enough Teshuvah? 54
Anger Is Energy 57
Histapkus vs. Consumerism and Entitlement 59
Repressed Anger 63
Tefillah BeTzibbur (Communal Prayers) 65

Do We Know What to Pray For?	67
The Meditation of Prayer	69
The Gravity of a Sin	73
Time Is Relative	75
Making Peace Among the Angels	77
Festivals for Joy	79
Let Your Fellow's Honor Be as Dear as Your Own	81
Succos — the Festival of Joy	83
Understanding Our Needs	85
I'm Here!	87
What's the Bottom Line?	89
The Great Value of Our Tefillah	91
Sin Against the Yetzer Hara?	93
Adam — A Unique Individual	95
The Lesson of Noah	98
Identifying the Voice	101
Bittul Hayesh (Self-effacement)	103
Strengthening One's Resolve	105
Not as Bad as Others	107
Sensitivity to Feelings	109
Making a Challenge "Bite Size"	111
Jacob and Laban	113
Not Angels	115
All Sins Are Theft	118
Simple but Pure	120
The World as a Mirror	122
Joy With Tremors	124
What's Major and What's Minor?	126
True Ahavas Yisrael (Love of One's Fellow Jew)	128
Psychological Blindness	130
Concepts of Tzedakah	132
The Pivotal Role of Self-Esteem	134
Hashem's Forgiveness	136
Justice With Chesed	138
The Ultimate in Hypocrisy	140

Empathy	142
Add to Your Mitzvos	144
The Cancer of the Internet	146
Guard Your Tongue	149
The Toxicity of Rage	151
Texting to Hashem	153
Poor but Worthy	156
More About Sensitivity	159
The Search for Truth	161
Do We Bless Hashem?	164
Emunah (Faith)	166
Fulfilling One's Potential	168
Tefillah (Prayer) Between Man and Hashem?	170
The Primacy of Simchah	172
True L'Shem Shamayim (Sincere Devotion to Hashem)	174
Simple Lessons, but Very Profound	176
Matzah and Chametz	178
The Dawn of Life	180
Gut Shabbos	182
The View From Above	184
Attitude and Behavior	186
Psychology and Judaism	188
Adapting to Adversity	192
Standards of Living	194
Our Plea for Life	196
A Unique Interpretation	198
Commitment	201
Alchemy: Fact, Not Fiction	202
How Is This Alchemy Accomplished?	204
A Cultural Insanity	206
Basic Chinuch	208
Wasted Opportunities	210
Everything Points to Hashem	212
Revivifying the Living	214
Sensitivity Toward Widows	216

Truthfulness	219
Brokenheartedness vs. Depression	221
Sharing Happiness	223
Forgiveness	225
The Ahavas Yisrael of a Zealot	227
Focusing	229
Determination	231
The Life of the World	233
Purim — the Eternal Festival	235
The Power of Stories	238
David — the Sweet Minstrel of Israel	240
Happiness	242
The Divine Gift	244
An Aveirah, Not a Mitzvah!	246
Authentic Torah Values	248
There's Enough Blame to Go Around	251
Descartes and R' Yeruchem	254
Declaration of Independence vs. Mesillas Yesharim	257
Discovering the Nucleus of Beauty	260
Kevod HaBerios (Human Dignity)	263
Appreciation	266
Life, Liberty, and the Pursuit of Misery	268
Rosh Hashanah vs. New Year	270
Keeping Secrets	272
Shalom Bayis and Who Am I	275
Cleaving to Hashem	277
Yiras Cheit (Fear of Sin) — Ahavas Hashem (Love of G-d)	280
Be Careful What You Pray For	282
Tefillah — Our Only Hope	284

INTRODUCTION

Time is mankind's most precious commodity. Lost wealth may be recouped. Money may be earned, acquired as a gift, or borrowed. Time cannot be acquired in any way. A moment that has passed is irretrievable.

It is for this reason that in many synagogues the interval between Minchah (afternoon prayer service) and Maariv (evening prayer service) has traditionally been used for Torah study. Some congregants study the *Mishnah*, and others study *Ein Yaakov* (the homiletic portions of the Talmud).

In our shul, the Minchah service takes place shortly before sunset, and the Maariv service a few minutes after sunset. There is thus a brief interval between the two services. In order to forestall these precious moments from being lost, our shul has opted to "seize the moments" and therefore it is the practice for someone to give a brief *dvar Torah* (Torah discourse).

On occasion it has been my privilege to be the speaker. These *divrei Torah* are nuggets of Torah wisdom culled from our vast Torah literature. It is my pleasure to share them with you.

At times, I use the prerogative of having the floor to apprise my listeners of psychological issues of which many are not aware. Although these are not strictly *divrei Torah*, I feel justified in using the opportunity to alert people to issues that are important to mental health. The Talmud often states that while something may not be a halachah (Torah Law), it is an *eitzah tovah* (good advice).

I have tried to impart *eitzah tovah*, and I have included these in this volume. It is up to us to "seize the moments" and utilize those spare minutes that arise during our day to learn Torah. As we say in the Shacharis prayer service on the Sabbath, "It is a tree of life for those who grasp it, and its supporters are praiseworthy" (*Proverbs* 3:18). "Its ways are ways of pleasantness and its paths are peace" (ibid. 3:17).

LIVING ACCORDING TO HALACHAH

Our great Torah personalities not only lived according to halachah, but every facet of their lives was regulated by halachah.

A man visited R' Chaim Ozer Grodzinsky of Vilna on Succos. R' Chaim Ozer, who was suffering from a cold, invited the man to eat in the succah. "I cannot join you," he said, "because I have a cold, and if one does not feel well, one is exempt from eating in the succah."

During the meal, the man was surprised to see R' Chaim Ozer entering the Succah, bundled in furs. R' Chaim explained, "It occurred to me that having a cold does exempt me from the mitzvah of succah. However, the halachah of *hachnassas orchim* [hospitality] requires that the host sit with his guest during the meal, and in the laws of *hachnassas orchim* there is no exemption for one who does not feel well."

When the Steipler Gaon was a conscript in the Russian Army, he stood sentry duty in the cold. Concerned that the coat he had been provided might contain *shaatnez*, he did not wear it until he felt that due to the cold he was at risk of *pikuach nefesh* (danger to life). He wore the coat until he felt the danger had passed; he then removed it, donning it again only when he felt that the severe cold presented a danger. He continued to alternate periods of wearing the coat and going coatless, according to his assessment of the risk to his life.

Some people think that halachah applies only to ritual laws, such as kashrus, Shabbos, etc. The Talmud states that the one brief verse on which the *entire Torah* depends is "Know Hashem in all your ways" (*Proverbs* 3:6). How we speak and relate to other people, including our immediate family members, is prescribed by halachah, as well as how we work and transact business.

One Shabbos, the Steipler Gaon insisted on going to a distant shul, although the walk was obviously taxing for him. He later explained that he had once noticed a young boy putting a volume of the Talmud on the bookshelf upside down. He gently told the child that this was disrespectful to a holy book. The child showed him that the volume had been bound incorrectly, and that he had indeed put it on the shelf right side up.

"I realized that I had wrongly reprimanded the child and asked his forgiveness. However, just as a minor is not halachically capable of transacting business, he likewise does not have the ability to grant forgiveness. Today is this boy's bar mitzvah, and he has, therefore, reached the age when he can grant forgiveness. That is why I had to go to that shul to ask his forgiveness."

When it was pointed out that he could have waited until after Shabbos and traveled by car, the Steipler Gaon said, "What assurance do I have that I will be here after Shabbos? Anything that one is obligated to do should not be postponed."

Thousands of people consulted the Steipler Gaon for advice. In the very last moments of his life, he wept bitterly, "Perhaps I may have given bad advice, which is a grievous violation of halachah."

That is living — and dying — according to halachah.

THE RISK OF PERSONAL INTEREST

The Torah relates that Korah led a rebellion against Moses, challenging Moses' Divine commission (*Numbers* Chapter 16). Rashi explains that Korah was angered because Moses had appointed a younger cousin, rather than Korah himself, as chief of the Levitic tribe; Korah therefore sought to disprove Moses' authority.

Korah was a great man, privileged to carry the Holy Ark when the Israelite camp was in transit. He had prophetic foresight. He had witnessed the miracles wrought by Moses in Egypt and the Splitting of the Reed Sea. He had seen that at Sinai, Moses had served as the intermediary between G-d and the Israelites. How could he have been so foolish as to challenge the validity of Moses' authority?

This teaches us the far-reaching effects of ego. Even a great personage, wise, honored, and imbued by the Divine spirit, is vulnerable to allowing his thinking to become totally distorted by an affront to his ego. Even the slightest personal interest can thoroughly mislead a person.

When a patient is prepared for surgery, his skin is carefully disinfected. If even a single bacterium, which can be detected only under microscopic magnification, escapes the disinfectant, this minuscule organism can propagate and result in the patient's death.

That is why the Talmud says, "Be very, very humble" (*Ethics of the Fathers* 4:4). Even the minutest ego sensation can warp the mind of the wisest of people.

Ego is probably the strongest human emotion. Let me share a personal anecdote.

> It often happens that a few days before Succos, one needs something for his succah from the hardware store. In Israel, there are hardware stores that can barely accommodate more than two customers. Two days before Succos, I was among several of the sardines in the hardware store, and a woman was arguing with the proprietor that the tape recorder she had purchased there was defective. The proprietor tried to convince her that she could return it to the manufacturer under the warranty, but she insisted that he must repair it and would not take "no" for an answer. The customers waiting for succah materials (and I among them) were seething with annoyance. It was all I could do to restrain myself from saying "Stop already! That tape recorder is not essential to the succah!" When she eventually stopped arguing, she turned around and noticed me.
>
> She said, "Oh, Dr. Twerski! I recognize you from your picture. I've read many of your books."
>
> Suddenly, my well-justified anger melted like butter on a hot stove. She had nourished my ego.

Watch out for your ego. It can make you do crazy things, as well as convince you to be inattentive to major mistakes, your own and those of others.

UNSUSPECTED THEFT

We are honest people, and we would never touch a nickel that belongs to others. However, there is a common form of theft of which one may be unaware: *gezeiles zman*, theft of time. If someone expects you at a given time, and you keep him waiting, you may be guilty of *gezeiles zman*. In fact, this may be more serious than theft of money, because for money there can be restitution, but there is no restitution for time that has been wasted.

> The Chazon Ish convened a *minyan* (quorum of ten men necessary for communal prayer) in his home, and one man said that he had an appointment. The Chazon Ish promptly sent him on his way, saying that forming a *minyan* at the expense of someone else's time was not permissible.

During the 1948 War of Liberation, there was a water shortage in Jerusalem, and there were long lines to obtain water brought to the city on water buffaloes. The wife of R' Isser Zalman Meltzer brought home several jugs of water and called to her husband to help carry them in.

"You returned very quickly," R' Isser Zalman said. "Were you allowed to go to the head of the line because you are my wife? If so, we cannot use the water, because it is the by-product of *gezeiles zman*." Only after she reassured him that she had stood in line and had not preempted anyone, did R' Isser Zalman consent to use the water.

It is wonderful to visit with friends, but one must always be cognizant of time: both yours and theirs. Therefore one should seek to arrive and depart in a timely manner. A friend who is invited for a specific hour should endeavor to be on time and not keep his host waiting (thereby wasting his time). He must likewise take into account that every minute of time is precious and should not overstay his welcome (your host may be exhausted or have something important to do). It is much better for friends to feel, "I wish they would have stayed longer," than "Are they never going to leave?"

When R' Yisrael of Salant visited Warsaw, the word spread through the city, and many people came to *daven* Minchah together with the *tzaddik* (righteous person). R' Yisrael *davened* uncharacteristically quickly. He later explained, "Some of them closed their shops to come here for Minchah. There was no justification to prolong their shops being closed."

Unsuspected Theft / 17

MANDATED LOVE

The Torah states, "V*e'ahavta es Hashem* — You shall love Hashem" (*Deuteronomy* 6:5). But love is an emotion. How can a person be commanded to have an emotion?

Rambam says that the mitzvah of *"ve'ahavta es Hashem"* can be achieved if one contemplates the wonders of creation. The commentary on the Rambam says that Rambam is defining *ahavas Hashem*. It can mean *love*, like that of a parent for a child or a husband for a wife, but it can also mean reverence. If one appreciates the infinite wisdom of Hashem as seen in Creation, one can achieve great admiration of Hashem, and this, too, is *ahavah*.

Rabbi Shneur Zalman provides two answers to the above question. In every Jewish *neshamah* (soul) there is *ahavah mesuteres*, a nucleus of love of Hashem that was bequeathed to us by the patriarchs Abraham, Isaac, and Jacob. This nucleus is concealed, because our indulgence in physicality and our lack of proper *middos* (character traits) obscure it. If a person abstains from excessive physical indulgence and refines his *middos*, the *ahavah mesuteres* is revealed and one will feel love for Hashem.

Rabbi Shneur Zalman also formulates the concept of "intellectual *ahavah*." If a person contemplates the greatness of Hashem and His many kindnesses, and understands intellectually that Hashem is deserving of love, he thereby fulfills the mitzvah of *ve'ahavta es Hashem*.

The Baal Shem Tov was asked: Inasmuch as Hashem is inaccessible to the senses, cannot be seen, touched or heard, how can one develop love for an abstract Being?

The Baal Shem Tov answered, "Love your fellow Jew, and you will develop love for Hashem." But this only pushes the question further. The Torah commands, "Love your fellow as yourself" (*Leviticus* 19:18). How can you be ordered to love someone? He either elicits your love or he does not.

Rav Eliyahu E. Dessler addresses this issue in *Michtav M'Eliyahu* (Vol. 1), pointing out the fallacy in the popular notion that you give to those whom you love. "It is just the reverse. You love those to whom you give." In this way, it is possible for a person to develop *ahavah* for another person by giving to him, primarily by doing acts of kindness to him.

Rav Dessler follows in the footsteps of earlier ethicists, beginning with the *Sefer HaChinuch,* which states that a person's emotions are affected by his actions. If you behave toward someone as if you loved him, you will grow to love him.

Which approach should one utilize to fulfill the mitzvah to love Hashem?

All of the above.

DEVELOPING EMOTIONS (I)

In his famous letter to his son, Ramban begins by instructing his son to control his anger, stating that this will lead to humility, which is the finest of all character traits.

If humility is the finest of all character traits, why did Ramban not instruct his son to be humble? Why did he tell him to achieve humility by controlling his anger?

Humility is an emotion, and one cannot be instructed how to feel. However, restraining oneself not to respond angrily when one is provoked is an *action,* and although one must exert great effort to control himself, that is something that is possible. Therefore, Ramban instructs his son to exercise control over an action, which will then lead to developing an emotion.

Ramban was not telling his son not to feel anger when provoked, because that is not under one's control. He was telling him not to allow himself to become overwhelmed with rage, something that is feasible, albeit difficult. If we are careful about acting properly, desirable emotions will follow.

If we eliminate one improper emotion, it has a ripple effect. It is much like the woman who replaced a shabby chair in her living room. The worn sofa looked out of place beside the new chair, and had to be reupholstered. Now the carpet was out of sync, and a new carpet was necessary, but the draperies were now incompatible. The entire living room was redecorated because of a single chair. It is much the same with character traits. A person who develops restraint of anger will find that other traits are incompatible, and these, too, will undergo change.

R' Shneur Zalman in *Tanya* states that the human mind is comprised of both intellectual and affective faculties. Physiologically, one is motivated by a desire of some sort, and one then uses his intelligence to satisfy that desire. The intellect is thus a tool of the affect. Because there is a desire for visual entertainment, the intellect was put to use to invent television. Because there is a desire for rapid communication, the intellect was put to use to devise jet planes, fax machines, and cellular telephones. Because people like tasty foods, the intellect is used to create recipes that will please one's palate.

Spiritually, R' Shneur Zalman says, the converse should be true. For a spiritual person, the intellect directs how he should feel. The intellect is a guide and teacher, rather than a tool of the emotions. Animals, too, have intelligence, and they use their intelligence to satisfy their bodily desires. Man should have enough pride to function at a higher level than an animal does. There are ways in which we can fashion emotion, but it necessitates determined effort. The Midrash says that "the heart [emotions] of *tzaddikim* [righteous people] are under their control, whereas the wicked are controlled by their emotions" (*Bereishis Rabbah* 34:1). We *do* have the ability to generate emotion.

DEVELOPING EMOTIONS (II)

As mentioned, it is possible to generate emotions by use of the intellect, but it requires effort. Of course, effort is the primary element in *avodas Hashem* (service of G-d). *Avodah* means *work*.

When the Rebbe of Zidachov was a child, his mother would touch his garments when he returned home from shul. If they were dry, she would admonish him, saying that he had not *davened* properly, because *tefillah* is an *avodah shebelev* (service of the heart). *Avodah* means *work*, and when you work, you sweat.

I don't know many people whose *davening* results in their sweating.

The *mussar* authorities say that we must use our imagination while *davening* and visualize scenes that will generate emotion. R' Shlomo Wolbe says that prior to reciting the *Shema*, when we say,

"You have brought us close, our King, to Your great Name," which refers to the Revelation at Sinai, we should envision the awesome scene of two million people surrounding Sinai, with the mountain trembling and aflame, with the cloud enveloping the mountaintop, seeing Moshe standing on the mountain, and we should hear the long sound of the shofar. Our imaginations can do this, just as it can create vivid Technicolor scenes when we dream. However, it takes time and meditation to conjure up the scene, and it is impossible to do so during the time the average *minyan* spends in prayer.

Similarly, when we recite the *Shirah* ("Song of the Sea") we should picture ourselves standing at the shore of the Reed Sea, having witnessed the miraculous splitting of the waters, crossing the seabed on dry land, and seeing the waters come together again to drown our ruthless enemies. Together with Moshe we sing praises to Hashem for this miraculous salvation. Again, this will take time and effort, but this enables us to recite the *Shirah* with passion.

There are numerous times when we should be using our imagination. The Haggadah states that it is mandatory that we personally feel the Exodus, and R' Yechezkel Levenstein says that we should use our imagination to recreate the scene of the Exodus and feel that we are among the freed Israelites. In the succah, we should visualize ourselves surrounded by the protective Clouds of Glory. On Rosh Hashanah we should picture ourselves standing before the Heavenly Tribunal, as our actions are being scrutinized. Who can envision such a scene without trembling?

The *sefarim* say that when we study Talmud, we should form a mental picture of the *Tannaim*, the *Amoraim*, and the commentators at our side. How different our learning would be if we would see ourselves in the presence of Abaye and Rava, with Rashi and Rambam standing before our very eyes.

Modern technology has impaired our ability to visualize. As a child, I listened to the radio, and had no difficulty in imaginatively experiencing the escapades of the Lone Ranger. Today's children not only waste precious time watching television or videos, but their imaginative skills have withered from the atrophy resulting from disuse. With time and effort, we can reinstate our imaginative faculties, and bring life into our *davening* and mitzvos.

Time and effort. These two concepts have become archaic in a world where the push of a button brings us immediate results. We must break away from this world of effortless, instantaneous gratification if we hope to find excitement and emotion in Torah, *tefillah,* and mitzvos.

THE POWER OF THE WORD

After a month of *teshuvah* (repentance) in Elul and Rosh Hashanah and the Ten Days of Repentance, we usher in Yom Kippur, the day of forgiveness, by reciting *Kol Nidrei*. What is *Kol Nidrei* about? It focuses on the cancellation of personal vows. Why is the possible violation of a vow so important that it takes priority over all other sins? Rabbi Elyashuv says it is because a vow is the result of a verbal statement, and we must realize the gravity of the spoken word.

The Chofetz Chaim dedicated his life to championing *shmiras halashon,* literally, "guarding our speech," so that we avoid *lashon hara* (defamatory speech), untruths, objectionable language, and conversing during prayers. The Talmud says that committing a sin creates an accusing angel (*Ethics of the Fathers* 4:13). This angel bears the nature of the sin. If one eats non-kosher food or violates Shabbos, while very serious sins, they do not involve speech; the resulting accusing angel is mute and cannot bring charges against the person.

However, if one commits a sin involving speech, such as speaking *lashon hara* or conversing during the services, the angel created thereby *can* speak, and it can cite all the sins that a person has done. In this way, the consequences of conversing during *davening* may be greater than those of more grievous sins.

In 1648, Chmelnitzky led a massacre of Jews in Eastern Europe. Entire Jewish villages were wiped out. Rabbi Yomtov Heller, author of *Tosafos Yomtov* on the Mishnah, attributed this calamity to the sin of people talking during services, and composed a special blessing (*mi sheberach*) for those who refrain from conversing during services.

At that time, there were Jews who did not observe Shabbos or kashrus. It would appear that these are more grievous sins than talking during the services, yet Rabbi Heller did not implicate these sins as the cause of the tragic events.

People are less careful of their tongues than of what they do with their hands. Yet speaking disparagingly about someone can destroy him just as if one had killed him.

It is customary to fast as penance for a sin. However, a *taanis dibbur*, keeping silent for a whole or part of a day, may be more meritorious, because it may enable a person to be more heedful of what he says.

There are many reasons why one should watch his speech. This is one more reason.

PERMISSIBLE REVENGE

Ramchal (Rabbi Moshe Chaim Luzzato) had a profound understanding of human nature, and refers to revenge as the "sweetest human emotion." Taking revenge soothes one's wounded ego, as well as being perceived as executing justice. Restraining oneself when the opportunity for revenge occurs demands considerable self-control. However, there is no choice: there is a halachic prohibition against taking revenge.

But the Torah requirement does not stop here. When the opportunity for revenge occurs, not only is it forbidden to say, "No way! You have the chutzpah to ask me for a favor after refusing me when I needed help," but it is also forbidden to say, "I'll do it for you even though you don't deserve it." If you are presented with an opportunity to do a kindness for someone, you are obligated to do so. The Torah is very explicit, "Do not take revenge or carry a grudge against your fellow" (*Leviticus* 19:18).

In addition to being a violation of Torah, carrying a grudge is simply foolish. It has been said that harboring resentment is "allowing someone whom you don't like to live inside your head without paying rent." Solomon said it very beautifully, "Anger lingers in the bosom of fools" (*Ecclesiastes* 7:9).

Yet there is a manner in which one is permitted to take revenge.

> The Chazon Ish, far from home, went into a village *beis midrash* and took a *Chumash* from the bookshelf. The *shammash* rudely snatched the *Chumash* from him, saying, "You're not a member here! You have no right to use these *sefarim* [holy books]."
>
> The following morning, when the *shammash* went around with the *tzedakah pushka* [charity box] to collect donations, the Chazon Ish put a paper note of a significant denomination into the *pushka*. The *shammash* looked at the donor, and realized that this was the person whom he had treated so rudely. He then brought a *Chumash* to the Chazon Ish.

> My father told a parable about a man who threw a rock at the king. The officers arrested him and he was to be severely punished, but the king intervened, pardoned him, and gave him a position in the palace. The man was remorseful. "Why did I throw a rock at so benevolent a king?" The king promoted the man, and with each promotion, he felt greater guilt and remorse.

The psalmist says, "May only goodness and kindness pursue me" (*Psalms* 23:6). Why is there pursuit? Who would run from goodness and kindness? King David is saying, "Hashem, if You wish to pursue me, it does not have to be with harshness. Like the king in the parable, You can punish me with kindness."

MODELING ADDICTION

Addictions, whether to drugs, alcohol, or gambling, are generally condemned. But what is addiction? It is a person's desire to get a pleasurable, momentary "high," even though the long-term effects may be disastrous to himself or to others.

But does mankind have a right to make such a judgment, when it destroys nature and pollutes the air and water, all for a momentary gain? Rain forests are wantonly razed and animal habitats are regularly destroyed, eliminating forms of life that can never be replaced, in order to profit from "civilized" developments. How is this different from the heroin addict?

The "greening" movement is a rather recent phenomenon. Over 2,000 years ago, the Midrash stated that when Hashem created Adam, He took him into the Garden of Eden and showed him all its nascent beauty. "I made all this for you," Hashem said. "Take care that you do not ruin My world, because there will be no one to repair it" (*Koheles Rabbah* 9).

Of course, it is possible to abuse even this "positive" ideal. The ultimate purpose of Creation was mankind, and those who give priority to the lives of whales, etc., to the detriment of humanity's needs are misguided and perverting the objective.

The recklessness with which we destroy nature sends a powerful albeit subtle message. Our youth is very sensitive, and readily picks up the message. "Do anything you want to for current gain, even though you will be ruining the world for yourself and for future generations."

There are other times when we do something for the momentary gain or pleasure, ignoring the long-term consequences. When a parent or teacher picks up a cigarette, he is modeling addiction for the children. Smoking has been declared an *issur* (forbidden) by the majority of halachic authorities. When directors of yeshivos turn a blind eye to their students smoking, not only are they essentially condoning an *issur*, but they are also approving frankly destructive addictive behavior.

Billions of dollars have been spent, unfortunately to little avail, to arrest the drug epidemic, notably among our youth. Perhaps if the adult world would practice self-control and stop living like addicts, sacrificing the long term for momentary gain, the kids would be less prone to do the same thing.

THE PRIMACY OF MIDDOS

There is a difference of opinion in the Talmud regarding the proper manner in which to recite the *Shema* upon retiring. The Torah says (to recite the *Shema*) "when you lie down and when you arise" (*Deuteronomy* 5:7). The school of Shammai takes this literally; i.e., to recite the *Shema* when reclining. The school of Hillel interprets this to mean, "*when* you lie down"; i.e., at bedtime.

In the Mishnah, R' Tarfon said, "I was coming on the road and I deliberately lay down to recite the *Shema* in accordance with the words of Beis Shammai. I thereby endangered myself on account of bandits." They [the Sages] said to him, "It would have been better for you to come to harm because you transgressed the words of Beis Hillel" (*Berachos* 10b).

The Jerusalem Talmud comments, "If R' Tarfon had neglected to recite the *Shema*, it would have been an omission of a positive commandment, which would not have been liable to physical punishment, but if he recited the *Shema* in a way that transgressed the words of Beis Hillel, he is liable by death! Why is this? Because he who breaks down a wall will be bitten by a snake [*Ecclesiastes* 10:8]" (*Berachos* 1:4).

In *Mussar HaMishnah,* R' Yehudah Leib Ginsburg suggests that the Talmud says that the schools of Hillel and Shammai had halachic disputes over a three-year period (*Eruvin* 13b). A *bas kol* (heavenly voice) proclaimed that the positions of both were true, but that the halachah follows Beis Hillel. Why? Because Beis Hillel were humble, and always cited the opinion of Beis Shammai before their own.

The Talmud says that Beis Shammai outnumbered Beis Hillel, and although Beis Shammai were *cherufim* (more keen), the ruling went according to Beis Hillel because their *middos* (character traits) were more pleasant.

The heavenly ruling in favor of Beis Hillel indicates that having fine *middos* is superior to extraordinary scholarship. The Talmud goes so far as to say that Torah knowledge that is not accompanied by refinement of *middos* can be toxic (*Yoma* 72b). R' Tarfon's adopting Beis Shammai's ruling indicated that he gave precedence to scholarship as being more important than fine *middos.* That is a grave error, and that is why he was subject to severe punishment.

R' Chaim Vital, the leading disciple of the Arizal, states that one must give *middos* even greater consideration than both the positive and prohibitive mitzvos. Although transgressing a Torah commandment is indeed a grievous sin, it does not become part of one's personality, and one may do *teshuvah* and attain forgiveness. An improper character trait, however, in ingrained in one's personality, and is much more difficult to eradicate.

THE MIRACLE OF THE HUMAN BODY

There is one prayer that is often not given its due. It is the prayer after one has taken care of one's bodily needs.

Blessed are You, Hashem, our G-d, King of the universe, Who fashioned man with wisdom and created within him many openings and many tubes. It is obvious and known before Your Throne of Glory that if but one of them were to be ruptured or one of them were to be blocked, it would be impossible to survive and to stand before You. Blessed are You, Hashem, Who heals all flesh and acts wondrously.

"Who fashioned man with wisdom and created within him many openings and many tubes." Each kidney is comprised of *a million tubes*! These tubes constitute the nephron, a condensed tubule. As the blood circulates through the kidney, the nephron filters the blood, extracting the minerals in the blood: sodium, potassium, chlorine, and other substances. The nephron then carefully *reabsorbs* just the right amount of these substances that the body needs, and excretes the rest.

People who experience kidney malfunction are non-functional and may survive with hemodialysis treatment several times a week, but the humble kidney performs this function 24/7/365 with an efficiency that even the finest hemodialysis equipment cannot duplicate.

It is worthwhile to take a course in human physiology just to marvel at the wondrous function of the kidney.

If one understands the phrase, "*Who fashioned man with wisdom*" in reference to the function of the kidney, one can then extrapolate to the infinite wisdom of the Creator Who fashioned man with a brain — *one hundred billion cells* that are multiply interconnected in a manner that is truly mindboggling. All the computers in the world combined could not approach the complexity of the brain, which carries out countless functions effortlessly.

My professor of neuroanatomy said that in those few seconds from the time the ball leaves the hands of the pitcher until the batter swings at it, hundreds of messages are sent throughout the central nervous system. Amazing!

How true are the words of Job, ""And from my flesh I can see G-d" (*Job* 19:26).

THE CHESED OF YIELDING

Rabbi Yitzchak Zilberstein relates the story of a young man who appeared to be living a charmed life.

The young man excelled in everything he did, was highly respected by his peers and teachers in the yeshivah, and made a wonderful *shidduch*. The rabbi of his shul said he knew why the young man merited this good fortune.

"When this young man was to become a bar mitzvah," the rabbi said, "there was another boy in the shul whose bar mitzvah was to be on the same Shabbos. Lots were drawn to determine which boy would have the ceremony at our shul. This young man won. The boy who lost was disappointed, because he would have to go to another shul, where most of the congregants did not know him or his family. This disconnect would diminish the joy in his *simchah*.

"The following morning, the winner said, 'I could not sleep all night, thinking about how sad this other boy is. Upon arising, I went to his home and told him he can have his bar mitzvah here and I will go to another shul.'"

The rabbi continued, "I have no doubt that Hashem is rewarding him for this act of *chesed* [lovingkindness]."

While yet in his youth, R' Akiva Eiger was renowned as a Talmudic genius, and was chosen as a *chassan* by a prominent individual. The prospective father-in-law invited the young Akiva for Shabbos and assembled the local scholars to meet him. To his dismay, Akiva did not say a *dvar Torah*, and when the scholars posed questions, he responded with one-word answers. They told the father-in-law, "You've been duped. He's not a genius. He's an ignoramus!" The man was so upset that he wished to break the *shidduch*, but Akiva said, "Wait just one day."

That Sunday, Akiva asked the father-in-law to reassemble the scholars, and Akiva delivered a four-hour profound Talmudic discourse, the likes of which they had never heard.

R' Akiva explained, "This past Shabbos, another *bachur* (young man; student) from our yeshivah was here; he had likewise become a *chassan* to a local family. If I had given my Talmudic discourse on Shabbos, the scholars would have compared this young man to me, and he would have felt slighted. That's why I waited until he had departed."

R' Akiva Eiger was a genius in *middos* as well as in Talmud.

TU B'AV — THE GREATEST OF OUR HOLIDAYS

The Gemara in *Taanis* 26b states that there were no *Yamim Tovim* for Israel like *Tu B'Av* (the fifteenth day of Av) and *Yom Kippur*. On Tu B'Av, in order to avoid embarrassing those who did not possess fine clothes, all the single daughters of Jerusalem would borrow white garments. They would don the borrowed clothing and go to dance in the vineyards, where the young men could observe them and select a bride. Young men were told, "Do not look for physical attractiveness, but look for the familial origin. 'Grace is false and beauty vain; a woman who fears Hashem, she should be praised' [*Proverbs* 31:30]."

We have all attended weddings, and we have heard the *berachos* (blessings) recited after the man and woman have become husband

and wife with the *kiddushin* effected by the giving of the ring. The first *berachah* is "*shehakol bara lichvodo* — everything was created for His [Hashem's] glory." This is indeed a wonderful concept, but have we ever given any thought to its relevance to the marriage ceremony? This sentiment would be in place on many other occasions, such as with the performance of any of the mitzvos, yet we do not recite it at other times. Our Sages surely had a reason for making it part of the marriage ritual.

The relevance of this *berachah* to marriage occurred to me at the airport. I was standing on the moving walkway, and an airline employee noticed a friend on the adjacent moving walkway, which was moving in the opposite direction. They could exchange only a few words, because they were soon out of each other's range.

Many couples who consult a marriage counselor are told that their problem is one of "communication," that they do not know how to communicate properly. It occurred to me that the two people on the walkways may have excellent abilities to communicate, but they could not put them to good use because they were heading in opposite directions.

This may also be true of marriage. The man might see the marriage as fulfilling *his* particular needs, and the woman might view the marriage as fulfilling *her* particular needs. If this is so, then they are heading in discordant directions, and their *shalom bayis* (marital harmony) is on a shaky foundation.

Our Sages, therefore, instruct the young couple that whereas every person has legitimate needs, the *primary* purpose of the marriage is to further *kevod Shamayim*, to establish a family that will bring greater glory to Hashem. When this serves as the foundation of the marriage, individual differences between husband and wife do not affect the basis of the marriage, and they may be reconciled more easily. If individual needs are primary, any frustration of one's needs undermines the very foundation of the marriage.

This requires an orientation that is alien to Western civilization, which is the most hedonistic in history. As I have frequently pointed out, Ramchal begins *Mesillas Yesharim* with "The Obligations of a Person in the World." Living a Torah life requires more than observance of the *halachos*; it requires that a person be driven by the will to do what Hashem wants, and this is the all-important purview of *middos*. Preoccupation with "what I want" will very likely encroach on what others may want, and in the close relationship of marriage may manifest as discord. Sometimes a couple may be so perfectly matched and their individual goals are so harmonious that no conflict of interest occurs, but this is indeed a rarity. Most often it is *ezer kenegdo*, a helpmate who may be oppositional in many ways.

Human beings are composite creatures, comprised of a physical body, which is essentially an animal body with all the drives characteristic of an animal, and a *neshamah*, which is G-dly in nature. Hashem created man and woman *betzelem Elokim* (in the image of G-d), and when both partners primarily seek to emulate Hashem and fulfill the *tzelem Elokim*, making the strivings of the *neshamah* primary, the frustrations that are often divisive in marriage are avoided.

The message of *Tu B'Av* makes it the greatest of all *Yamim Tovim*. "Grace is false and beauty vain; a woman who fears Hashem, she should be praised." When a relationship is based primarily on personal gratification, it is "false and vain," void of the components that can make it an enduring and happy marriage.

Never before in Jewish history has the incidence of failed marriages been so high, with tragic consequences to both partners and catastrophic effects on their children. We are derelict in not having a true perspective of what a Torah-true marriage should be like, and the young men and women who are taught Torah in yeshivos and seminaries are woefully unprepared for marriage.

We must teach our sons and daughters that the goal of marriage is *shehakol bara lichvodo,* and the most effective way of impressing them with this is by modeling our marriages for them. Just think what *nachas* you will have when your children have healthy, happy marriages, because they are united by striving toward a common goal, *shehakol bara lichvodo.*

GUILT VS. SHAME

uilt and *shame* are not identical.

Healthy guilt can be constructive. Healthy guilt is the feeling one has when one has done something wrong. This feeling can lead to *teshuvah* (repentance), to making amends and paying restitution. It is also a deterrent, in that one will avoid doing something that will result in the distressing feeling of guilt. Guilt is a statement concerning an *action*.

Shame, on the other hand, is not about an act, but about a *person*, stating that the person rather than the act is bad. If one feels that for whatever reason, one is inherently bad, then there is nothing one can do about it. *Teshuvah* is not effective for shame. Repenting and atoning for an act are not going to change the composition of the person; hence, someone experiencing shame either does not do *teshuvah* or, if he does, is not thereby unburdened. To put it another way, guilt is, "I made a mistake," whereas shame is, "I *am* a mistake." If a person has done adequate *teshuvah* and still feels "guilty," he is probably dealing with shame.

King David says, "Because I admit my iniquity, I worry because of my sin" (*Psalms* 38:19). R' Nachman of Breslov commented, "My iniquity is that I constantly worried about my sin." This worry can be paralytic, preventing a person from constructive behavior.

The prophet says, "I have erased your sins like a fog that has cleared" (*Isaiah* 44:22). When a fog clears, not a trace of it remains. When one has done adequate *teshuvah*, one should feel free of the burden of sin. R' Mendel of Kotzk said, "Sin is like mud. Whichever way you handle the mud, you get dirty." Repeatedly thinking about the sin can be contaminating.

Because shame is toxic, parents should be cautious not to inflict shame on children. It is necessary to discipline a child and tell him, "What you did was wrong," but not "You are bad," or "You are lazy." Negative statements about what one *is* can have long-term harmful effects. Since children believe these statements, that can be ruinous to their self-esteem. When my father disapproved of something I did, he would say, "You are too good for that. Such behavior is beneath your dignity."

Children assume that their parents are right; children will believe what their parents say about them. Parents should be careful with their words.

KOSHER MONEY

Yes, money can be as *tereifah* as *tereifah* foods. Money that is acquired dishonestly is *tereifah*. The Talmud says that if a person steals wheat, grinds it into flour, bakes it into bread, and recites the *Hamotzi* when eating it, he angers Hashem. "This is not a *berachah;* it is blasphemy" (*Bava Kamma* 94a).

Giving *tzedakah* and paying a child's tuition in a yeshivah are indeed great mitzvos, but only when one comes by the money honestly.

When the Torah was given at Sinai, the people "saw the voice" of Hashem (*Exodus* 20:15). The Midrash states that this was a miracle, in that they were able to see sound, which is normally heard rather than seen. Someone asked R' Yitzchak Meir of Gur (*Chidushei HaRim*) what purpose this miracle served.

R' Yitzchak Meir responded, "The Hebrew word *'lo'* has two meanings. When it is spelled with an *aleph,* it means 'not,' but when it is spelled with a *vav,* it means, 'to him' or 'for him.'

"When Hashem said *'lo signov,'* He meant 'You shall not steal,' because this was *lo* with an *aleph*. However, the spoken *lo* could be mistaken as *lo* with a *vav,* which could be misunderstood to mean, 'for Him you may steal,' which would sanction doing mitzvos with money that was acquired dishonestly. It was, therefore, necessary for the people to see the spoken words, so that they would know that *lo signov* means 'You shall not steal.'"

The acquisitive drive is one of the most powerful human emotions. Some desires fall away with advanced age, but the desire for money never disappears. Because it is so powerful, people are prone to rationalize and justify how they acquire their money.

> A known thief in Brisk married off a daughter, and people asked R' Chaim whether they may eat the food at the wedding feast.
>
> R' Chaim asked the thief, "What would you do if you had the opportunity to break into a *tereifah* meat market?"
>
> "I would do so," the thief answered.
>
> "And if it were on Shabbos?" R' Chaim asked.
>
> The thief said, "Rebbe, that's how I make my *parnassah* [livelihood]."
>
> "And would you steal the meat?" R' Chaim asked.
>
> "Of course," the thief said.
>
> "And what would you do with the meat?" R' Chaim asked.
>
> "I would sell it to non-Jews," the thief answered.
>
> "Wouldn't you eat it?" R' Chaim asked.
>
> The thief was horrified. "Rebbe," he said, "What do you take me for? I'm a Jew! I would not eat *tereifah* meat."
>
> R' Chaim lamented. "How tragic that meat can be regarded as *tereifah,* but stolen money can be considered to be kosher."

Kosher Money / 43

TRUTH AND HUMILITY

The Maggid of Mezeritch was asked, "The psalmist says, 'Truth will sprout from earth' (*Psalms* 85:12). If truth is readily available, why is falsehood so prevalent?"

The Maggid answered, "Truth is indeed on the earth, but people are reluctant to bend down to pick it up."

Vanity and falsehood go together. The ultimate truth is that the only real existence in the world is Hashem. If one realized this, one would be in a constant state of self-effacement.

> One of the *tzaddikim* was accorded great honor by his admirers. He said that every time someone praised him, he felt a pain as if he were stabbed with a knife.
>
> He explained, "A king once wanted to see how his subjects lived. He

knew that if he went among them as a king, they would not act as they normally do. Therefore, he dressed in civilian clothes, and took a minor official to accompany him. Wherever they went, people stood up in respect for the official, who was distressed by the honor accorded him. "These people don't know that the king is walking beside me. If they knew who he really is, they would show him great honor and respect and totally ignore me."

How can a person be vain if he is aware that he is always in the presence of Hashem? One would feel himself to be even less than nothing.

Humility can enable a person to have *simchah* (joy). In the Yom Kippur liturgy we say that although Hashem receives praise from the holy heavenly angels, he prefers the prayers of us lowly mortals to that of the angels. One should feel greatly honored by this privilege, that one's prayers are desired more than those of angels.

> R' Elimelech of Lizhensk said, "I am confident of being admitted to Gan Eden. The Heavenly Court will ask me, 'Melech, did you study Torah adequately?' and I will say, 'No.' They will say, 'Did you *daven* properly?" and I will say, 'No.' They will say, 'Did you give adequate *tzedakah?"* and I will say, 'No.' They will say, 'He is truthful. Let him into Gan Eden.'"

Truth and humility go together.

PRAISE OF GRATITUDE

In *Psalms* we read, "A song for the Shabbos day. It is good to thank Hashem and to sing praise to Your Name" (*Psalms* 92:1-2). *Bnei Yisasschar* asks, "What is so special about praise on Shabbos? In the *Amidah* [*Shemoneh Esrei*] prayer, we say, 'Everything alive will gratefully acknowledge You.' We always praise Hashem, not only on Shabbos."

Bnei Yisasschar cites the words spoken by the matriarch Leah when she bore her fourth son, Yehudah. She said, "This time let me gratefully praise Hashem" (*Genesis* 29:35). The Talmud comments that from the time the world was created, no one had expressed "grateful praise" to Hashem before Leah. Although we find earlier expressions of praise to Hashem, we do not find the term "grateful praise" until Leah used it.

The reason for this is that "grateful praise" applies when one has received an extra bonus of kindness. Thus, prophetically knowing that Jacob would father twelve sons, Leah assumed that inasmuch as he had four wives, each would be blessed with three children. When her fourth child was born, she said, as Rashi quotes, "I have received more than my share," and for this extra kindness, she expressed "grateful praise."

We know that the reward for mitzvos is reserved for the Eternal World, as the Talmud says, "We do the mitzvos today, but the reward will come tomorrow, i.e., in the future" (*Eruvin* 22a). Nevertheless, Hashem has given us the Shabbos, which is a "taste" of Gan Eden, so that we can experience some of the eternal reward even in this world. This is a gratuity, an extra gift that Hashem has given us, and for this extra gift we offer grateful praise to Him.

With this we can better understand the words of the Mussaf prayer of Shabbos, "Those who delight in it [Shabbos] will inherit everlasting honor," referring to the eternal reward in Gan Eden, but "those who savor it will merit life," meaning that they will have a taste of the eternal bliss in this world.

A LOUD BUT SILENT CRY

The Torah relates that when Pharaoh's daughter went down to bathe at the Nile, she saw the basket among the reeds. When she opened it, she "saw him ... a youth was crying" (*Exodus* 2:6). Would it not have been more correct to say that she *heard* the child cry? The answer is that Jews know how to cry silently.

In the High Holy Days prayers we say that at the Heavenly Tribunal, "a great shofar is sounded, and a small, still voice is heard." R' Nachman of Breslov said that you can literally scream with a soundless "small, still voice" but no one will hear it, only you.

R' Nachman said, "Just imagine the sound of such a scream in your mind. Depict the shout in your imagination, exactly as it would sound. Keep this up until you are literally screaming with this soundless 'small, still voice.'"

When you picture this scream in your mind, the sound actually rings in your brain. You can stand in a crowded room, screaming out to Hashem in this manner, and no one else will hear you."

We recite the *Amidah* silently, so as not to disturb other worshipers. But the pain we feel in our prayer, whether for relief of personal suffering or that of *Klal Yisrael* (the Jewish People) in exile, can result in a loud scream, heard by no one else but Hashem.

BEWARE OF OFFENDED PRIDE

The Torah relates that Hashem accepted Abel's offering favorably, but rejected Cain's offering. Cain was angry and disappointed; Hashem said to him, "Why are you angry and why has your countenance fallen?" (*Genesis* 4:4-6). One of the commentators asks, "What is the meaning of Hashem's question? It is obvious that Cain was upset because his offering was rejected."

He answers, "Hashem's question was, 'Tell me the truth, Cain. Are you angry because your offering was rejected or because Abel's was accepted?'"

This is just one of the many Torah insights into human nature. A person may be able to tolerate his own loss, but cannot tolerate that someone else won.

> It is related that a butcher had a cow slaughtered, and a *she'ailah* (halachic query) was discovered. The Rav's ruling rendered the meat *tereifah*. The butcher accepted the ruling without reaction. At a later date, the butcher had a dispute with someone about a paltry sum and when the Rav ruled in favor of the other party, the butcher became enraged at the Rav. His monetary loss at the ruling of *tereifah* was much greater than that of the dispute, but in the former case, although he lost, no one else had won. In the latter case, even though his loss was a fraction of the previous ruling, what bothered him was that the other person had won.

Hashem knew the real reason Cain was upset. It was not that his offering was rejected, but that Abel's was accepted.

This is an important insight. We may indeed be upset by adversity, but if it affects our ego, our reaction is more intense.

During the financial recession, many people who lost their jobs reacted with depression. The same person, had he quit his job, would not have reacted this way, although the financial loss was no different. This is because when one quits a job, one has made the decision himself and it is not a narcissistic pain, whereas when one is laid off, this is not only a financial loss but also a blow to one's ego. It is not "something that I did" as when one quits his job, but rather, "something that was done to me."

Every person has pride, and when something happens that affects his pride, he may act to defend it. So much rides on our ego involvement that when we feel attacked, our better judgment may fail and we may do things that we do not recognize as being self-defeating.

We must be exceedingly cautious about how we act when we assume that our pride has been attacked.

TOO GOOD TO BE GOOD

The Torah states that at the end of the sixth day of Creation, "G-d saw all that He had made, and behold! It was very good" (*Genesis* 1:31). The Midrash states, "*Tov* [good]; that refers to the *yetzer hatov* [Good Inclination]. *Tov me'od* [very good] refers to the *yetzer hara* [Evil Inclination]." The commentaries struggle with this cryptic Midrash. Why does *tov me'od* refer to the *yetzer hara*?

The Maggid of Dubno explained with one of his noteworthy parables.

> In those days, there was no refrigeration, and meat that was more than a day or two old would be on the verge of spoiling and would develop a bad odor or taste. The innkeepers would spice the meat heavily with fragrant spices that masked its foul odor and unpleasant taste. Those attracted by the fragrance enjoyed the meat. However, wise people

understood that the heavy spicing was intended to hide the fact that the meat was actually spoiled.

The Maggid said that Hashem created the world and provided man with the essentials for life. However, Hashem wants man to exercise his free choice between good and evil. Man would be rewarded for choosing to do good; Hashem therefore created evil, which He wishes man to avoid.

Of course, if a person would recognize that something was evil, he would shun it. Hashem, therefore, "spiced" evil heavily, to make it attractive to man. Foolish people, attracted by the enticing "fragrance" of evil, partake of it. The wise person realizes that if something appears to be so desirable, it must be that it is actually detrimental, and that its alluring attractiveness is the "spice" that masks its true evil nature.

This is what the Midrash means. If something in Creation appears to be *tov me'od*, watch out! That may indicate that in actuality it is bad, and precisely for that reason was made to appear preferable to that which is good.

In my many years of treating drug addiction, I saw how true this is. There are few things in the world that are as destructive as cocaine and heroin. Yet, their lure is forcefully compelling.

This is why Moses said, "I have placed life and death before you, blessing and curse; and you shall choose life" (*Deuteronomy* 30:19). Why was it necessary to instruct the Israelites to choose life and blessing? It is because death and curse are so heavily spiced that people think them to be good. Only the wise discern the deceptiveness of their attractiveness.

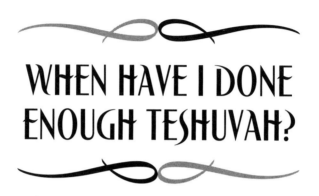

WHEN HAVE I DONE ENOUGH TESHUVAH?

I received the following query.

> With Yom Kippur approaching, a problem I have regarding *teshuvah* is resurfacing.
>
> In an incident a number of years ago, my foolish and irresponsible behavior ruined my career. I have agonized over it, and have tried to do everything I'm told to do to achieve forgiveness, but the guilt has never left me. How can I know when my teshuvah has been complete?

This was my response.

Rambam says that if a person committed a sin and did *teshuvah*, and then finds himself in the identical circumstances in which the sin occurred, but this time avoids committing the sin, this is effective *teshuvah*. But such repetition of identical circumstances may not occur. No angel is going to come down and tell you that your *teshuvah* is complete, so how can you know?

You say that you are trying to achieve forgiveness. We know that if one does sincere *teshuvah*, Hashem surely forgives him. Perhaps it is time for you to accept this and stop agonizing over the past.

Some aspects of *teshuvah* may appear to be contradictory. Moshe Rabbeinu says, "You will return to Hashem," and then repeats, "You will return and hearken to the voice of Hashem" (*Deuteronomy* 30:2). Why the repetition?

The answer is that a person who commits a sin is generally blind to the wrong that he is doing, because that is how the *yetzer hara* operates, blinding one to the evil of the sin. When one begins to do *teshuvah*, he begins to see the true nature of the sin, and when he does so, this stimulates him to do more intense *teshuvah*. The latter further increases his awareness, so that he is constantly increasing his *teshuvah*.

> Rav Saadia Gaon was at an inn, but the innkeeper did not know who he was. When the host discovered his guest's identity, he apologized, saying, "I'm sorry. I did not know who you were and I did not accord you the respect due you. If I had known who you were, I would have treated you with greater respect."
>
> Rav Saadia began to weep. "Yesterday, I served Hashem to the best of my ability, according to my knowledge of Him. Today I have greater awareness of Hashem, and if I had known yesterday what I know today, I would have served Hashem better."

As we do *teshuvah*, our awareness of the gravity of a sin increases, stimulating us to do further *teshuvah*. That is why the Torah repeats, "You will do *teshuvah*, and that will lead you to do further *teshuvah*."

But this increased awareness of sin should not depress us. *Teshuvah* should be done with *simchah*. We should recognize our human frailties and be on the alert so that the *yetzer hara* does not trap us. But we should know not only that Hashem forgives us, but that as we

When Have I Done Enough Teshuvah? / 55

do *teshuvah*, as Rambam says, we become more dear to Hashem. Our increasing efforts at *teshuvah* make us more beloved to Hashem, and that is reason for *simchah*.

ANGER IS ENERGY

Management of anger is one of the most difficult challenges a person faces. It is evident that anger is energy, because explosive anger obviously releases a great deal of energy. However, such rage is inevitably destructive. The Midrash relates that on three occasions Moses became angry, and each time, he erred (*Vayikra Rabbah* 13:1). The Talmud states "Anger causes a wise man to lose his wisdom and a prophet to lose his prophetic powers" (*Pesachim* 66b).

Some people mistakenly think that if they hit a punching bag or do similar actions, they are discharging their anger. There is no psychological validity to this. To the contrary, this may intensify their anger.

The Rebbe of Gur (*Imrei Emes*) was accompanied to the train station by his chassidim. He said to them, "Do you know why that engine can pull so many heavy cars? It is because it contains the steam and channels it to the pistons and wheels." The Rebbe was teaching the chassidim that the internal "steam" the body generates, i.e., anger, can be productive when channeled properly.

People often have a knee-jerk reaction, responding angrily when provoked. Discharging their anger this way may give them an immediate sense of relief, but the long-term effects are invariably negative. Once the rage reaction is set in motion, logic can no longer prevail. "The wise man loses his wisdom," and one may do something foolish he will later regret.

It is crucial to pause when provoked. Even a brief pause can allow one to think.

Anger is generally due to one of three things: hurt, fear, or frustration. Think, *Why did this event or this person make me angry?* Next, think, *What result do I want to achieve?* Next, think, *What is the best way of getting what I want?* If you can contain the "steam," as the train engine does, and manage to process these three thoughts, you may be able to put the energy of the anger to constructive use. You will be able to experience pride instead of regret.

HISTAPKUS VS. CONSUMERISM AND ENTITLEMENT

"He afflicted you and let you hunger, and He fed you the manna" (*Deuteronomy* 8:3).

"Lest you eat and be satisfied, and build good houses and settle" (ibid. 8:12).

My forty years of working in addiction demonstrate the truth of the statement of Ramchal in *Mesillas Yesharim*: We must be most cautious that our "wants" do not become "needs" (*prishus*). The core of addiction — whether to drugs, alcohol, gambling, food, or whatever else — is that a *desire* for something, which a person could at one time decide whether or not to gratify, can become so intense a *need* that a person may do anything and everything to gratify it. The cocaine or heroin addict will do whatever is necessary to obtain the drug: cheat, steal, and yes, one may even kill.

> Some Holocaust survivors came to Israel with only the clothes they were wearing. Our shul held a clothing drive and we sent many bundles to Israel. One of the "thank-you" letters we received was written on the recipient's personalized stationery. I asked my father how a person who is so destitute could afford personalized stationery. He explained that before the war, she had been very wealthy. To her, personalized stationery had become a necessity, not a luxury.

That is what has happened to many people in today's society. There are two major influences that affect us: *consumerism* and *entitlement*. Consumerism is an industry wherein the media are used to make us believe that there are things that we *must* have. A prime example of this is seen when children carry on that they *must* have a particular doll or toy that was advertised. In order to preserve their sanity, the parents relent and buy it for them. Invariably, within a few days the doll or toy will end up on the heap of other "absolutely necessary" toys in the closet.

While we may not be able to fault the juvenile mind, the fact is that many adults are taken in by consumerism and are convinced that various material items are vital to their existence.

> The Steipler Gaon once asked his students to come to his home for the *shiur*, which he delivered while lying in bed. He was not ill, but he had only one pair of trousers, which were at the tailor.

The second operative principle nowadays is *entitlement*. Many people believe that they are entitled to what others have, *even if they have not done anything to earn it*. When I was a child, we had no air-conditioning, microwaves, washer-dryers, cell phones, and many other material possessions that are in common use today. It is obvious that these are not actually necessities of life. However, they have become necessities. If people earn enough to afford these luxuries, they may certainly have them. However, there are able-bodied people who are recipients of charity and who believe that they are *entitled* to these extras. To deny them these things is considered as heartless as if they were denied food, clothing, or shelter.

The Steipler Gaon said that in his childhood, candy was a rarity. A fresh apple was a treat, and the "new suit" for Pesach was a hand-me-down that had been altered to fit, and a child was thrilled to receive it. Today, many children feel that they are entitled to everything, and if they do not get what they feel thay are entitled to, they are unhappy and angry. This attitude persists into adult life, and the Steipler Gaon believed it is a leading cause of much unhappiness.

Many Jewish families live below the poverty line, and are in need of food and rent money; it is the greatest mitzvah to help them. But many people have become immersed in a lifestyle consisting of much more than their basic needs, and their children feel that they are entitled to similar standards.

Numerous scholars study Torah with great dedication and true *mesiras nefesh*. It is difficult to live according to the literal meaning of the mishnah, "This is the way of Torah: Eat bread with salt, drink water in small measure, sleep on the ground, live a life of deprivation — but toil in the Torah" (*Ethics of the Fathers* 6:4), but many adhere to a frugal lifestyle.

> The wife of one kollel *yungerman* was asked, "Don't you have a husband? We never see him at *simchos*."
>
> She answered, "My husband has a set *seder* (schedule of study sessions) and says that he is not being paid to go to weddings."

The conclusion of the above-cited mishnah in *Ethics of the Fathers* is, "If you do this, you will be happy in this world and it will be good for you in the World to Come." R' Simchah Zissel said that if one only observes how others live in greater comfort, one cannot be happy in this world. But "*If you do this,*" i.e., if you indeed live frugally, you will achieve happiness.

I enjoyed a close relationship with the Steipler Gaon; I can tell you that he was a happy person. His home had the very barest of furnishings, but he was far happier than some people who live in luxury.

However, there are some *bachurim* who have been influenced by the prevailing *entitlement* and *consumerism* attitudes. Their expectation of a *shidduch* is that the father-in-law will provide expensive living quarters and furnishings as well as a comfortable stipend. This is inconsistent with the statement, "The Torah was given to be studied only by those who ate the manna" (*Tanchuma Beshalach* 20). Obviously the Torah was given to all future generations, but the Midrash means that the Torah was given to be studied by those who live a frugal life, such as existing on the rations of the manna.

Is it possible that some young women cannot make a *shidduch* because their fathers are unable to meet the boys' demands? If this is so, it is a most serious indictment. Sodom was destroyed because of the complaints of one young woman.

We must take care to avoid being influenced by the prevailing attitudes in our environment. The message of consumerism is that "without this, you cannot be happy." Falling prey to consumerism is dangerously similar to the bottomless pit of drug addiction, where there is never any gratification that endures for more than minutes. Indeed, many youngsters who have fallen into the trap of drugs were looking for the happiness of which consumerism convinced them they had been deprived.

Many of the *sifrei mussar* emphasize the importance of *histapkus*, being satisfied with the basic necessities. This is a counterculture attitude, in direct opposition to the consumerism and entitlement attitudes. However, even some in the *frum* world do not adhere to *histapkus,* which is an important principle of living a true Torah life. We would do well to examine our values to see whether they are really consistent with Torah values.

REPRESSED ANGER

If one has done as was recommended in a previous essay, he has taken potentially destructive energy and utilized it wisely. However, one must have an awareness of what he is dealing with.

A psychological mechanism known as *repression* is a process that takes place in the subconscious mind. "Subconscious" means that the person has no awareness of it. For any of a variety of reasons, the repressive mechanism may cause a person to be unaware that he is angry. In the same way, some conditions of nerve damage result in a person not being able to feel pain. Such a person may sustain a burn and not be aware of it. This is what repression can do. A person may be unaware that he is angry. The anger is stored deep in the subconscious mind, where it can fester and eventually manifest itself negatively.

One cannot channel the energy of anger into constructive channels unless he knows it exists. Repression of anger makes one unable to do this.

> It is related that the Chofetz Chaim used to pray tearfully at the open *aron kodesh*, asking that Hashem relieve him of feelings of anger. The Chofetz Chaim was never enraged, but *feelings* of anger are innate and not subject to one's control. Since having these feelings bothered him, he asked Hashem to remove them. Obviously, the Chofetz Chaim was aware of his angry feelings. Had they been repressed, he would not have had knowledge of them and would not have been able to beseech Hashem to remove them.

Repressing anger is not a virtue. One should be aware of its existence and deal wisely with it.

TEFILLAH BETZIBBUR (COMMUNAL PRAYERS)

The Talmud holds *tefillah betzibbur* in high esteem, saying that Hashem never turns away *tefillah betzibbur*. Yet, although we so often *daven* in a group, we may not find that our prayers are answered as we expressed them. Numerous commentators relate that although we do not see the results we desire from our prayers, they nevertheless do have a beneficial effect. One of the commentaries says that *tefillah betzibbur* does not mean that a number of people pray in the same room, but rather that all are praying for the same thing. There may be one thousand people praying in one room, but, according to this opinion, if each one is praying for his own personal needs, that is not *tefillah betzibbur,* the prayer of the *tzibbur*, but rather that of a thousand individuals, each praying for himself.

The Talmud says that one who answers *Amen* to another person's *berachah* has even greater merit than the one who recited the *berachah*. This is because when one recites the *berachah* thanking Hashem for being able to see, to walk, and to have clothes or other needs, one is grateful for what Hashem gave to him. However, one who answers *Amen* to the *berachah* is expressing his gratitude for what Hashem gave to the *other* person, and gratitude for the good fortune of others is of greater merit than one's gratitude for the gifts he himself receives.

The Arizal writes that prior to *davening* in the morning, one should say, "I hereby take upon myself fulfillment of the mitzvah *ve'ahavta lerei'acha kemocha* [to love one's fellow as oneself]. Of course, just reciting the words does not mean much. One must sincerely commit to loving others. This makes our *tefillah* extraordinarily potent.

The Midrash says that unity among Jews is so dear to Hashem that He is willing to withhold punishment even for idolatry if they are united.

In several places in *tefillah,* we say *b'shem kal Yisrael*, that we are doing the mitzvah in the name of all Israel. Sharing the merits of *tefillah* with all of Israel makes our prayer *tefillah betzibbur.*

DO WE KNOW WHAT TO PRAY FOR?

My mother used to say, "When the *kallah* [bride] and the *chassan* [groom] stand under the *chuppah* [wedding canopy], this is their Yom Kippur! All of their sins have been forgiven, and their prayer is so propitious. Do they know what to pray for? There are so many challenges that they may face in the years ahead. But they are children, and they have no idea what to pray for."

My mother would often tell me, "When you took your first steps, we were overjoyed. We clapped our hands. 'Look! He is walking!' And I picked you up and kissed you.

"An itinerant rabbi, who goes about collecting for charity, was present. He shook his head sadly and said, 'When I started to walk, my parents were happy, too. But now when people see me walking toward them, they're not at all happy.'"

My mother responded, "When a child begins to walk, the parents should pray that he should grow up to be a person whom people will be happy to welcome."

We do not always utilize the opportunity to pray effectively. The Talmud says that when the Holy Temple was destroyed, all the gates to heaven were closed, except for the gate of tears. This gate is open for tearful prayers.

A Chassidic rebbe asked, "If the gate of tears is always open, then what is the purpose of having a gate there?" He answered, "The gate is there so that it can be shut when one cries foolishly."

Yes, there can be foolish prayers. The beautiful letter from Ramban (Nachmanides) to his son prescribes rules for daily conduct. At the end of the letter, Ramban writes, "Read this letter once a week, and on the day you read it, whatever you pray for will be granted."

Well, I tried it and it didn't work. I read the letter and prayed to win the lottery, but I didn't. My disappointment abated when I realized that it did not even occur to Ramban that after being inspired by his letter to greater spirituality, anyone would be so foolish as to pray to win the lottery. He assumed that the person would pray for Divine guidance to achieve a closer relationship to G-d, or things of that nature. That kind of prayer would be granted. My prayer to win the lottery was foolish, and that is not what Ramban intended.

THE MEDITATION OF PRAYER

"When a person meditates in fields, all the grasses join in his prayer and increase its effectiveness and power" (*Likkutei Maharan* II, 11).

Meditation is an ancient spiritual discipline designed to encourage contemplation and mindfulness. In its many forms, meditation can induce relaxation as well as improve concentration and awareness, ease anxiety, and encourage authentic personal reflection unencumbered by the ego. With practice, meditation can help us find happiness within ourselves, as well as deepen our relationships with others and with Hashem.

Meditation is often thought to be exclusive to Eastern religions. Some people who are interested in developing a disciplined meditation practice visit Asia or seek out Eastern teachers of meditation. But there is no need to search for meditation in other places when it can be found in Judaism.

There is abundant evidence for the role of meditation in Judaism, beginning with Torah literature. The Talmud states, "The pious of yore would meditate for one hour preceding prayer and for one hour following prayer" (*Berachos* 30b). Chassidic writings stress the importance of *hisbodedus* (seclusion) and *hisbonenus* (meditation). Chassidic masters were known to go into the woods and meditate for hours at a time.

As further evidence of the practice of meditation in Judaism, Rambam describes the prophets' state of mind when they received their prophecy as a meditative state wherein they eliminated all distractions, all earthly concerns. The foremost interpreter of the *Zohar*, R' Yitzchak Luria (the Arizal), was known to go out to the field to welcome the Shabbos meditatively. Tourists in Safed can visit the synagogue that was built on the spot where the Ari welcomed the Shabbos.

In the vast repertoire of Chassidic music we find melodies of devotion known as *deveikus nigunim* that are conducive to meditation. In some Chassidic enclaves, the third Shabbos meal, held late in the afternoon, is extended into the evening. In the dark, with no distractions, *deveikus nigunim* are sung and the participants meditate.

Prayer is also a form of meditation.

My great-grandfather told us of a chassid whose meditation during prayer was so profound that he said, "I was afraid his soul would attach itself to Hashem and not return to him. To save his life, I interrupted his meditation and removed the *tefillin* [phylactery] from his head." That is the intensity that meditative prayer can reach.

Unfortunately, prayer that is recited by rote is stripped of its meditative quality. To restore the contemplative aspect, many Torah leaders advocate that after reciting formal prayers, we should pray spontaneously, composing our own prayers. A champion of this was the Chassidic master, R' Nachman of Breslov.

R' Nachman cited the verse from *Song of Songs*: "Come, my Beloved, let us go into the fields, let us lodge in the villages. Let us wake at dawn. Let us see if the vines have budded or the pomegranates have blossomed. There I will display my love for You" (*Song of Songs* 7:12-13). R' Nachman would pray, "Master of the universe! May I merit to enjoy seclusion, to regularly go into the fields among the trees and grass and all the vegetation, and to pray. This will be prayer between me and my Creator, to speak out everything that is in my heart, and all the grasses and trees will join with me and lend their power and vitality to my words and prayer, until my prayer will be with the utmost perfection as they elevate their spirit and life force to their supernal source. Thereby, I will be able to open my heart in abundant prayer and supplication and pour out my heart like a flowing stream before You in holiness, and lift my hands to You in prayer for my soul and the souls of my children" (*Likkutei Tefillos*).

Spontaneous prayers can be deeply meditative, but they can be difficult to practice when we feel pressured to rush through the service and get on with our day. It is a mistake to think that meditation can be achieved only under special conditions. No appurtenances are needed.

You may spend the next eight hours communicating with others. You have earned two minutes to be in touch with yourself. Before turning on the ignition in your car, close your eyes, take a few deep breaths, and shut out the world. You are alone with yourself, and, of course, in the presence of the Omnipresent God. Think something along these lines: *Master of the universe! Show me the way to achieve Your will. Do not allow the events of the day to distract me from fulfilling Your mission for me.*

An alcoholic may stop off for a drink before work, to artificially and destructively alter his state of mind. You can develop a more peaceful mind-set naturally, by dedicating yourself to fulfilling Hashem's mission for you, which is to become the best person you can be. The many interactions and transactions of the day, the successes and even the failures, need not distract you from your goal in life.

The Meditation of Prayer / 71

Before going to a business lunch, close the door of your office for 5-10 minutes of meditation. You will be eating to give your body the calories and minerals it needs. Give your soul the nutrients it needs. You may say, "But I have such a tight schedule." Yes, I know. My schedule as a doctor was also tight, but I found time by using "the president's room."

What is "the president's room"?

> A man drove up to a large motel with a neon sign reading, "No vacancy." Nevertheless, he requested a room.
>
> The clerk said, "Didn't you see the sign, 'No vacancy'?"
>
> The man said, "Don't tell me that if the president of the United States came in, you would not find a room for him."
>
> The clerk said, "Well, for the president we would have to find a room."
>
> The man said, "Good. The president is not coming. You can give me his room."

The message of "the president's room" is that if some emergency arose, one would find time. If, on the way to lunch, you twisted your ankle and could not walk, you would go for help. Fortunately, you did not twist your ankle, so use a bit of the time you would have spent caring for your painful foot to care for your own spirit.

It is helpful to read books on meditation (e.g., *Jewish Meditation,* by R' Aryeh Kaplan) and develop advanced meditative skills, but realize this. If something goes wrong at work, and a transaction or an investment that you hoped would be profitable came to naught, you would likely brood over it. *Brooding is nothing other than negative meditation,* which is at best, useless, and at worst, destructive. If you know how to brood (and who doesn't?) you can turn it around and meditate positively, making your day productive.

THE GRAVITY OF A SIN

It is a *mitzvah d'Oraisa* (Biblical commandment) to blow the shofar on Rosh Hashanah, and the enormous importance of a mitzvah need not be stressed. Yet, if Rosh Hashanah falls on Shabbos, we do not blow the shofar. Why not? Because one who does not know how to blow the shofar properly may carry the shofar to a Rav to be taught how to blow it; by carrying the shofar in a public thoroughfare, he will violate the prohibition of carrying on Shabbos. The Talmud explains that the Sages have been given the power to do away with the performance of a Scriptural mitzvah in a passive manner; i.e., by restricting its performance.

This is truly striking. Violating the halachah against carrying in a Biblically defined public thoroughfare is not a common occurrence, and the odds of one carrying the shofar there to seek instruction makes it even more unlikely. Yet, the remote possibility that a rare individual may accidentally violate Shabbos is something so serious, that for the past 2000 years, millions of Jews have been deprived of fulfilling a Scriptural mitzvah.

Penicillin has saved millions of lives, yet, over the years, thousands of people have died because of an allergic reaction to penicillin. But despite the latter, penicillin has not been withdrawn from the market. Even today, there are approximately 400 penicillin-allergy deaths each year. The probability of a fatal reaction to penicillin is far greater than that a person will carry a shofar through a Scripturally forbidden thoroughfare. To avoid that unlikely sin from happening, the Sages saw fit to eliminate blowing the shofar on Shabbos. That shows us their understanding of the gravity of a sin.

Penicillin remains on the market because the number of lives that it saves overwhelms the number of deaths it will cause. But the gravity of a sin is so great that the remote possibility that one may inadvertently sin is not overpowered by the fulfillment of the mitzvah of shofar many millions of times over the past two thousand years!

The Sages of the Talmud instituted many regulations to prevent a person from inadvertently committing a sin. This is because they understood the gravity of a sin. We would be wise to share this understanding.

TIME IS RELATIVE

R' Mordechai of Lechovitz said that a chime clock is a very helpful instrument. Each time it chimes a quarter-hour, it reminds you that another segment of time has irrevocably passed, and it prompts a person to make an accounting of his life.

We might benefit from having chime clocks. How many people spend hours watching inane programs, allowing valuable time to go to waste? Yes, there is a place for judicious entertainment, but even healthy things can be toxic if used to excess. Vitamins and minerals are essential for health, but megadoses can cause serious damage.

> At an acquaintance's house, I saw an 11-year-old child with a brilliant mind spend two hours consecutively watching cartoons. What a shameful waste of a bright mind! It has truly been said that killing time is not murder. Rather, it is suicide.

A chime clock can also bring joy. R' Ber of Ropschitz lodged at an inn, and asked the innkeeper where he had purchased his chime clock. "Every time it chimed," he said, "I felt like getting up and dancing."

The innkeeper said that a traveler had not had money to pay his bill, so he left the clock as security.

"Was he possibly related to the Seer of Lublin?" R' Ber asked.

"Now that you mention it, I do recall that he said something about the Seer of Lublin."

"I knew it must be so," R' Ber said. "You see, a chime clock can be depressing, indicating that a portion of life has irretrievably passed. But the Seer's clock always communicated that we are getting ever closer to the Ultimate Redemption. That is why it made me feel like dancing."

Time is relative. It can be depressing, but it can also be exhilarating. It depends on how we look at it and how we use it.

MAKING PEACE AMONG THE ANGELS

On returning from shul on Friday night, we greet the angels that escort us home by chanting the traditional "*Shalom Aleichem* — Peace upon you, ministering angels." However, the actual welcoming mentioned is not until the second verse, "*Bo'achem Leshalom* — May your coming be for peace." What, then, is intended by the *Shalom Aleichem* in the first verse?

Furthermore, in the first verse, we address "the ministering angels," but we do not repeat this description in the remaining three verses. Obviously, the first verse is not directed at the angels that escort us. Why do we say, "Peace upon you," to them?

The Midrash states that when Hashem said, "Let us make man" (*Genesis* 1:26), He consulted with the angels in His decision whether to create man. The angel of *chesed* was in favor of man's creation, because man would do *chesed*. The angel of *emes* (truth) opposed man's creation because man is disposed to falsehood. The angel of *tzedek* (justice) was in favor, because man is just. The angel of peace was opposed, because man is prone to quarreling (*Bereishis Rabbah* 8). There was thus a disagreement among the ministering angels.

On Friday night, we inaugurate Shabbos with the verse, "The heavens and the earth were finished, amid all their array" (*Genesis* 2:1). Rashi says that when Shabbos begins, we should consider everything we had to do as having been completed (*Exodus* 20:9). We don't owe anyone any money, and no one owes us any money. All the expected merchandise has arrived, and all the orders have been filled. Nothing has been left undone. There is nothing to worry about. We observe Shabbos with joy and absolute trust in Hashem.

When the ministering angels who opposed the creation of man see how we observe Shabbos, they admit that they were wrong. Man is indeed a wonderful creation. They no longer dispute his creation. Hence, *Shalom Aleichem*, the ministering angels have made peace.

FESTIVALS FOR JOY

In our prayers on the festivals, we say that Hashem has given us *moadim lesimchah*. This does not mean just "joyous festivals," but festivals that should serve as a source for joy all year round. If we celebrate Pesach, Succos, and Shavuos properly, with their full meaning, we can derive teachings that will provide joy throughout the year.

However, we must do something to sustain the joy of the festivals, lest we be like the "wise men" of Chelm.

> The wise men of Chelm wanted to save several rays of the summer sun to provide warmth in the winter. They put barrels of water in the sunlight to capture the sun's rays, then they closed the barrels tightly and stored them in the cellar. In the winter, when they opened the barrels, they were disappointed to find that the water had frozen and had retained no heat at all.

We cannot store the joy of the festivals in barrels. After Pesach, we must remember that we were liberated from slavery, and that we should not only be free of enslavement to a tyrannical despot, but that we should not be enslaved by forces within us. A person who is addicted to alcohol, drugs, food, gambling, cigarettes, or making money is very much a slave to these internal drives. We should celebrate our liberty and preserve it.

After Succos, we should remember that just as Hashem protected us in the Wilderness with Clouds of Glory, so he protects us throughout our lives. After Shavuos, we should carry with us the inspiration of receiving the Torah. Indeed, we are told that every day we should consider the Torah as fresh and as new as if we had received it just that day.

On the festivals, it was mandatory to make a pilgrimage to the Temple in Jerusalem. Just think of what it was like when millions of people from all corners of Israel met in Jerusalem, renewing old friendships and bonding in the service of Hashem. We can do this all year round.

The festivals are indeed *moadim lesimchah*, a source of joy throughout the year.

LET YOUR FELLOW'S HONOR BE AS DEAR AS YOUR OWN

One Friday, R' Moshe Kliers, rabbi of Tiberias, was advised that the *eiruv* (symbolic fence that permits carrying in a public thoroughfare on Shabbos) had broken, and that it was repaired according to the directions of the Sephardic rabbi, but that the repair may not have been adequate. R' Kliers investigated the problem, and ruled that carrying was permitted that Shabbos.

On Sunday, R' Kliers visited the Sephardic rabbi. "I've been studying the Talmudic laws on *eiruv*," he said, "and there is one passage in the Talmud that I cannot understand. Perhaps you can look at it and explain it to me."

The Sephardic rabbi said, "Surely, you jest. You don't expect me to have a better understanding of the Talmud than you."

"Nevertheless," R' Kliers said, "I may just be overlooking something, and a fresh perspective might reveal it."

The two studied the portion of the Talmud together, and in their discussion, the Sephardic rabbi said, "But something like this occurred just this past Friday, and I see that my ruling was wrong."

R' Kliers said, "I was apprised of it, and that's why I wanted to get your opinion."

"Well, what did you tell the people about the *kashrus* of the *eruv*?" the Sephardic rabbi asked.

"I told them that it was permissible. You see, in Tiberias, carrying in the public thoroughfare is a Rabbinic and not a Scriptural violation even if there is no *eiruv*. However, disparaging a person's honor is a Scriptural violation. Had I said that your ruling was wrong, that would have reflected poorly on you.

"Now you have the opportunity to correct your ruling without embarrassment."

(from *Hizharu Bichvod Chavreichem*)

SUCCOS – THE FESTIVAL OF JOY

It is generally assumed that the joy of Succos was paramount due to its falling at the time of harvest, when the people happily gathered the bountiful crops for which they had toiled the past six months. But there is another reason for the joy of Succos.

The Torah instructs us to celebrate Succos by living in temporary dwellings for seven days, "So that your generations will know that I caused the Children of Israel to dwell in booths when I took them from the land of Egypt" (*Leviticus* 23:43). The prevailing opinion in the Talmud is that Succos commemorates the miracle of the Clouds of Glory that surrounded the Israelites during their sojourn in the Desert and protected them from the rocky terrain, wild beasts, serpents, and the torrid sun.

There were two additional great miracles during the 40-year sojourn in the Wilderness: the manna that descended upon the encampment six days a week with a double portion on Friday, and the well of Miriam, that supplied water in the arid Desert. Yet, the Torah does not command us to commemorate these two great miracles, only that of the Clouds of Glory.

Bnei Yisasschar cites *Chida* who explains that the manna and the water were provided to the Israelites when they demanded them. This indicated that their *bitachon* (trust) in Hashem was lacking. After witnessing the wondrous ten plagues in Egypt and the Splitting of the Reed Sea, they should have understood that Hashem would not allow them to starve. However, they did not ask for the protective Clouds of Glory. They were unaware that this was even possible. The Clouds of Glory were Hashem's gift to protect them, and indicated that Hashem provides for His people far more than they expect.

This is a message of faith and *bitachon*. A person who feels certain that Hashem will tend to his needs will indeed do reasonable *hishtadlus* (effort), but will not be overwhelmed with anxiety and worry about the future, and will be free to enjoy whatever he has.

The Succos message of the Clouds of Glory facilitates having *simchah* not only during the festival, but every day of the year as well.

UNDERSTANDING OUR NEEDS

Most people think that they know what their needs are, and if their needs were met, they would be satisfied and happy. The things for which we pray are a good indication of what we feel we need: health, *parnassah* (livelihood), wisdom, and *nachas* (pleasure) from our children.

R' Elimelech of Lizhensk composed a "Prayer Before Prayer." If we would understand that one of our needs is prayer, then we would pray for the ability to pray.

In this prayer, R' Elimelech says, "Help us see only the good in others, and not their faults." R' Elimelech thus states that seeing only the good in other people is a human need, and we should pray for it just as we pray for other needs.

Just think of it! We need food, clothing, shelter, and good health. But even if these basic needs and a few others were met, we may still not be happy, and we may not know why. Unfortunately, there are people who are consistently unhappy and therefore they may act foolishly in the hope of finding happiness. Some may turn to drink or to drugs, some may seek the high of gambling. People may blame their unhappiness on a variety of things. One may believe that his job is causing his unhappiness and he will switch jobs. Another may think that a new car or a new home will make him happy. Most often, acquiring these things may provide temporary relief, but when the novelty wears off, his discontent returns. I know of cases where people attributed their unhappiness to a spouse, and actually divorced in the hope of finding happiness.

R' Elimelech's prayer makes an important statement. Seeing only the good in other people and not seeing their shortcomings is a human need! If a person lacks an essential need, he cannot really be happy.

While prayer is certainly effective, we should make an effort of our own to achieve that which we pray for. We ask Hashem for *parnassah*, but we must make an attempt to earn our livelihood, and that is when we can expect Hashem to answer our prayers. Similarly, we should make an effort to see the good in others and to look away from their faults. This is one of our needs, and meeting this need may be a vital key to happiness.

I'M HERE!

I should have listened better to what I was praying.

One day, as I was watering the lawn, a car pulls up and two men jump out. "How are you doing, Doc?"

The men were two recovering addicts who were alumni of my Gateway Rehabilitation Center. Inasmuch as I happened to be downcast that day, I bypassed the usual social response of "Just fine, thank you," and said, "I've got a bummer day today."

"You need an AA meeting, Doc," they said.

"No, thank you," I said. "I'm not for a meeting today."

At 8 p.m. the doorbell rang. It was these two guys. "We're here to take you to a meeting, Doc."

I appreciated their intentions and went along with them.

The meeting happened to be a "gratitude meeting," at which people relate how long they've been sober and how wonderful life is now that they are no longer drinking or using drugs. One person after another related how happy he or she was now. Inasmuch as I was downhearted, hearing how happy everyone else was did little to lift my spirits.

The very last person to speak said, "I've been sober for four years, and I wish I could tell you that they've been good. My company downsized and I was let go. I haven't been able to find a job. My wife divorced me and has sole custody of the kids. I fell behind in my mortgage payments and the bank foreclosed on my house, and last week the finance company repossessed my car. But I know that G-d didn't bring me all this way just to walk out on me now," and with that he sat down.

I knew why I was at that meeting. The way I was feeling, I needed to hear that.

The following Shabbos I was reciting the *Nishmas* prayer, and read, "You redeemed us from Egypt, Hashem, our G-d, and liberated us from the house of bondage. In famine You nourished us and in plenty You sustained us. From sword You saved us, from plague You let us escape, and from severe and enduring diseases You spared us. Until now Your mercy has helped us, and Your kindness has not forsaken us, and You will not abandon us, Hashem, our G-d, forever.

"*Until now Your mercy has helped us, and Your kindness has not forsaken us, and You will not abandon us, Hashem, our G-d, forever!*" Of course!

"I know that Hashem didn't bring me all this way just to walk out on me now."

I had been reciting that prayer for decades, but never heard what I was saying! "I'm here now, and the reason I'm here is because Hashem has taken care of me. He certainly is not going to abandon me now."

That transformed my mood, and every Shabbos, when I read *Nishmas*, my conviction is reinforced that Hashem is not going to walk out on me now.

WHAT'S THE BOTTOM LINE?

On the first Shabbos after Succos (*Shabbos Bereishis*), my father would relate the following story:

A Chassidic Rebbe took the goblet of wine to make *Kiddush* on Friday night, and closed his eyes in meditation. But rather than stand in contemplation for a few minutes, he maintained that posture for several hours. The goblet of wine fell from his hand, and the chassidim fell asleep at the table. When he finally roused himself, he made *Kiddush*, then explained to his chassidim:

"When a merchant goes to the *yarid* [commercial marketplace], he is completely occupied making transactions, buying and selling, and he does not have the opportunity to summarize what he has accomplished. In the evening, when he goes to the inn to rest, he takes out all his bills of sale and receipts and calculates what he achieved that day.

"From the beginning of Elul, I have been constantly busy with *teshuvah*, divesting myself of sins and bad *middos*. This continued through *selichos,* Rosh Hashanah, *tashlich,* the intervening days of *teshuvah, kapparos,* and Yom Kippur. I acquired mitzvos, the mitzvah of *teshuvah,* observing the *Yamim Tovim,* shofar, fasting, Succos, the four species, Simchas Torah. During this time I was too busy doing these things to make a calculation.

"This Shabbos was my first opportunity to make an accounting of what I had accomplished during the past seven weeks. That's why I had to spend so much time meditating."

We should all be making an accounting. Think of how tragic it would be if the merchant, after making his calculations, found that the bottom line showed no profit. Then all his efforts at the *yarid* were futile!

After the various aspects of *teshuvah* and the many mitzvos we did, what is our bottom line? Is our *davening* any better now? Is our Torah study any better? Have we refined our *middos*? It is to be hoped that we will find that we did indeed profit from all our actions in the past seven weeks.

THE GREAT VALUE OF OUR TEFILLAH

Rebbe Noach of Lechovitz said that a king may be entertained by the finest musicians. Indeed, he may order an entire orchestra to play for him if he wishes. Yet, in his throne room there may be a cage containing a tiny songbird, a creature that cannot read musical notes and knows nothing about composers and orchestration. This tiny bird's song may be more pleasing to the king than that of the most sophisticated musicians.

Similarly, Hashem has myriads of holy angels who sing His praises, but as we say in the *tefillah* of Yom Kippur, the praises that we mere mortals utter are dearer to Him than those of the mighty angels.

The Baal Shem Tov said that when a Jew comes home from work, realizes that it is almost sundown, and cries, "*Oy*! I was afraid I might miss the time for Minchah!" and *davens* quickly, the angels in heaven tremble before the *kedushah* (holiness) of his prayer.

Angels are indeed very holy, but they are not subject to the stresses and worries that beset humans. When we shrug off our stresses and worries and devote our hearts to Hashem in *tefillah*, our prayers surpass those of the angels.

Although there is much we should do to improve the quality of our prayer, we may take heart from a comment by the Chofetz Chaim.

> The Chofetz Chaim said that when farmers bring their grain to the market in times of plenty, the merchants examine the grain to determine its quality and to see how much earth and gravel might be intermixed with the grain. In the event of a famine, when grain is scarce, no one checks the grain. Whatever the farmers bring is immediately bought.
>
> "So it is with prayer," the Chofetz Chaim said. "In bygone years, when there were many *tzaddikim* whose prayers were pure and sincere, Hashem would distinguish between the prayers and hold them to a higher standard. Today, when there are so few *tzaddikim*, there is a scarcity of pure, unadulterated prayers, and Hashem is nonetheless accepting of our prayers, although they fall short of the ideal.

SIN AGAINST THE YETZER HARA?

In the *Al Cheit* (confession prayer) of Yom Kippur we say, "For the sin we committed with the *yetzer hara*." That is a bit strange. Aren't all the sins committed with the *yetzer hara*?

We may understand this with a parable from the *Zohar*.

> A king wished to test the fortitude of the prince, so he engaged a woman to beguile the prince. The woman did her utmost to fulfill her assignment, but in her heart she wished that she would fail. She hoped the prince would be firm enough in his faith and moral principles to resist her attraction.

The *yetzer hara* has an assignment. Hashem commissioned it to entice us to sin, and it fulfills its duty to the best of its ability, it really wants us to resist it. When we give in to its temptations, it has indeed succeeded in its task but feels bad about it. So when we give in to the *yetzer hara,* we actually disappoint it. That is what is meant by "For the sin we committed with the *yetzer hara.*" When we sin, we actually offend the *yetzer hara.*

> In a somewhat similar parable, a king wished to test the loyalty of his subjects, so he hired someone to foment revolution and incite people to disobey the king.
>
> Those who fell into the trap were punished.
>
> Others argued against this person, telling him that the king's rules were just. However, because he had succeeded in engaging them in a discussion, he used the opportunity to convince some that they were wrong and turned them against the king.
>
> The wise people, however, said, "How could it be that so mighty a king would allow someone to foment rebellion? Obviously, this person must be an agent hired by the king just to test us." Therefore, they saw no purpose in listening to him and arguing with him, and just sent him on his way.

Hashem has absolute rule over the entire world. Why would He tolerate a *yetzer hara* that tells us to disobey Him? Obviously, he allows the *yetzer hara* to perform its duties in order to test our loyalty to Him. Knowing this, there is no purpose in getting into a discussion with the *yetzer hara,* because it is shrewd enough to convince us that what it is suggesting is really not disobeying the King. The best thing, therefore, is simply to ignore it and send it on its way.

ADAM — A UNIQUE INDIVIDUAL

During Creation, Hashem had the earth bring forth a multitude of creatures, and there were many of each species. Adam, however, was created as a single individual. The Midrash asks why man was created as a single individual, and gives several reasons.

Perhaps one reason is that Hashem intended each person to be unique. "Just as their facial features are unique, so are their minds unique" (*Tanchuma Pinchas* 10).

I recall people whom I knew back in the 1930s. These were people who emigrated from Eastern Europe early in the 20th century, and they were fiercely unique. These people's thoughts were not shaped by the mass media or by educational institutions; hence, each one's personality was as unique as his fingerprints and DNA. Each person thought for himself, yet there was surprisingly little disunity.

Today, we vote in blocs and think in blocs. We are influenced by the mass media, major corporations, and the leaders of educational institutions. Indeed, the educational system has been criticized as forcing all students into the belly of the bell curve, resulting in mediocrity as well as uniformity. We yield to whatever fad prevails. Our thoughts are formed by everyone except ourselves.

There are indeed rules and principles by which we must all abide, but there is ample room within these parameters to be oneself. What is *my* goal in life? What do *I* think happiness is? What are *my* unique abilities that I should develop? What kind of lifestyle do *I* want?

> Rebbe Shalom Shachna, the father of the Rebbe of Rizhin, married the granddaughter of Rebbe Nachum of Chernobel. The latter's chassidim did not approve of Rebbe Shalom Shachna's ways, which did not comply with the Chernobel practices, and the chassidim complained to Rebbe Nachum. When Rebbe Nachum asked his grandson why he was not conforming, the latter answered with a parable.
>
> The egg of a duck was placed together with the eggs of a hen. When the chicks hatched, the mother hen took them for a walk. As they were passing a stream, the duckling jumped in. The mother hen panicked, shouting, "Come out of there! You'll drown!"
>
> The duckling responded, "Have no fear, Mother. I know how to swim."
>
> Rebbe Nachum told his chassidim, "Leave him alone. He knows what he is doing." Rebbe Shalom Shachna was the ancestor of the dynasty of Rizhin, renowned for its uniqueness.

Read the words of Rav Shlomo Wolbe.

> *Like Adam, every individual is an entire world. The existence of billions of people does not detract from each person's uniqueness. Every individual is a one-time phenomenon.*
>
> *Every person should know, "I, with my strengths and talents, facial features and personality traits, am unique in the world. Among all those living today and in all past generations, there*

was no one like me, nor will there ever be anyone like me to the end of time. Hashem has sent me into the world with a unique mission that no one else can fulfill, only I in my one-time existence" (Alei Shur Vol. 2. p. 71).

How distant from reverence for Hashem is the person who seeks only the approval of others, and is ready to imitate whatever he sees others do" (Alei Shur Vol. 1. p. 132).

Perhaps only tangential yet not irrelevant is a phenomenon I have observed. If one asked my older brothers where they were learning, they would say, "By Reb Shlomo," referring to HaRav Shlomo Heiman of Mesivta Torah Vodaath. Others would say, "By Reb Aharon," referring to HaRav Aharon Kotler of Lakewood. Others would say, "By the Rav," referring to HaRav Yosef Dov Soloveitchik. If you ask a yeshivah *bachur* today where he learns, he answers, "In Ponevezh," or "In Brisk," or "In Tchebin," or "in YU." Students identify with a *place* rather than with a *person*.

It may be more convenient to follow the herd instinct. That spares us the need to think for ourselves. However, if happiness is the result of self-fulfillment, we may be sacrificing happiness for convenience.

THE LESSON OF NOAH

The Torah is not a history book. "Torah" means "guide," and everything in Torah is intended to guide us.

After emerging from the ark, "Noah debased himself and planted a vineyard. He drank of the wine and became drunk" (*Genesis* 9:20-21). What does this teach us?

"Noah was a complete *tzaddik*" (ibid. 6:9). How does a "complete *tzaddik*" drink to intoxication?

The commentaries say that Noah knew how much he could imbibe safely without the wine affecting him, but that was before the Flood. What Noah did not take into account is that the world had undergone a radical change, and it was not the same world he had known. In a new world, old rules may not apply. What was tolerable in the old world may not be tolerable in the new world.

In the 16th century, R' Chaim Vital, primary disciple of the Ari z"l said, "Given the pollution of the environment, our only hope is prayer." He was not referring to carbon dioxide pollution, because there were no automobiles then, but rather to the spiritual deterioration. If the spiritual atmosphere of the 16th century was polluted, what can we say about our present-day environment, when the airwaves convey gross immorality, violence, and corruption into our living rooms! Every trace of decency has been eroded. Every day, new scandals about people in positions of leadership are revealed.

Our world has undergone a radical change. Not only is it not the world of yore, but it is not even the world of decades past. The old rules are not adequate. Some human foibles were tolerable in the old world, but today we must live by higher standards. In past generations we could live as *Shulchan Aruch Yidden*, and that was good enough, but today we must be *Mesillas Yesharim Yidden* to give ourselves and our children the spiritual capital necessary to survive the current spiritual atmosphere.

R' Chaim Vital felt that prayer was a solution. Perhaps we should become a bit more sincere about our prayer. Prayer requires meditation, but how much can one meditate when the most desirable *minyan* is the one that finishes fastest?

In the past, young people married and raised families, and for the most part, families were stable. Today we have a divorce rate that is alarming, and children are affected by the deterioration of *shalom bayis*. Our young men and women are marrying without the slightest concept of the new responsibilities that are part and parcel of marriage, and that consideration for one's partner must override one's own wishes. There is an unprecedented hemorrhage of our children deviating from the ways of their families and turning to drugs and other destructive lifestyles. Parenting by instinct is not acceptable. Young people, single and married, should be educated about marriage and parenting.

Most parenting is done by modeling. We must work diligently on refinement of our *middos* in order to resist the noxious effects of today's hedonistic world, in which we are essentially trying to go up on the "down" escalator.

While the challenges presented by today's world are daunting, we are assured that *"ha'ba l'taheir misay'ein oso* — one who comes to purify himself is given assistance [from Above]" (*Yoma* 38b). Hashem helps us overcome all challenges, and thus no challenge is insurmountable. But to merit that help, we have to *"ba l'taheir"* — we must do our best to purify all aspects of our lives.

The lesson of Noah is that when the world has changed, we cannot afford to continue "business as usual." We must take concrete steps to improve ourselves, our *tefillah*, our marriages, and our children's spiritual environment and opportunities.

IDENTIFYING THE VOICE

When you hear the voice of someone you know well, you can identify the person by the sound of his voice just as if you saw him.

Sfas Emes says that this is what happened at Sinai. "All the people saw the sound" (*Exodus* 20:15). Rashi says that they were seeing the impossible: that which is audible rather than visible. Our *neshamos* (souls) are part of Hashem, as the Torah says, "He blew into his nostrils the soul of life" (*Genesis* 2:7), and as *Zohar* points out, "One who exhales breathes out from within himself." Hence the expression, "[He] blew into his nostrils the soul of life," means that Hashem instilled part of Himself within man. Our *neshamos*, which were in the immanent presence of Hashem before we were born, know well the voice of Hashem, and when they hear the voice of Hashem they can identify Him as if they had seen Him.

The experience at Sinai is indeed unique. The Israelites reached a level of spirituality never attained heretofore, and we are very distant from that level. Nevertheless, we do have a *neshamah* that is part of Hashem, and we should be able to recognize His voice.

The Talmud says, "Every single day a heavenly voice emanates from Mount Horeb [Sinai], proclaiming and saying, 'Woe to them, to the people, because of [their] insult to the Torah'" (*Ethics of the Fathers* 6:2). The Baal Shem Tov asks, "What purpose does this voice serve if we cannot hear it?" He answers that although the voice is not audible to the human ear, the *neshamah* hears the voice. When a person has a moment of spiritual inspiration, it is because at that moment the *neshamah* has heard the voice of Hashem.

Our physical body, however, does not wish to acknowledge this voice, because this would deter the person from the things that the body craves. The body, therefore, seeks ways in which to render us oblivious to this voice.

The body seeks comfort. It is a common experience that when the alarm clock rings, we dream of a scene in which there is the ringing of a bell. The mind concocts this scene to disguise the true nature of the ring, so that our sleep will continue uninterrupted. It is amazing that within a fraction of a second, with the very first sound of the bell, the mind can create a whole scene into which the ring seamlessly fits. That is how cleverly the mind can operate. However, the persistent ringing of the bell ultimately breaks through the defense of the dream and we wake up.

Unfortunately, unlike that of the alarm clock, the voice from Sinai is not persistent. It makes its brief proclamation and becomes silent. If we are not alert to it and seize upon it, we miss the opportunity. Therefore, Ramban says that when we feel a spiritual inspiration, we should immediately do something to reinforce it, such as to give *tzedakah*, to study Torah, or to recite verses from *Psalms*.

Like out ancestors at Sinai, we are privileged to hear the voice of Hashem. We should not allow our bodily desires to prevent us from hearing it.

BITTUL HAYESH (SELF-EFFACEMENT)

I am not at all satisfied with the translation of *bittul hayesh* as "self-effacement," but I have not found a better translation. *Bittul hayesh* may be best understood as selflessness, the opposite of "narcissism." The latter is a condition in which a person's ego is out of control. He thinks himself to be the greatest and expects everyone to recognize it. *Bittul hayesh* is not only humility, but also realizing that one exists solely to fulfill the mission for which he was created, which is to develop spirituality and become close to Hashem.

The consciousness of self of the narcissist is, in fact, a kind of mental illness. Think for a moment about where your ears are, then your eyes, then your throat. If you do not make it a point to deliberately think of them, you would not be aware of them; that is, as long as you are healthy and they are functioning well. If something does call your attention to them momentarily, they quickly slip out of your awareness. Being conscious of part of your body generally means that there is something wrong with it. It either hurts or is not functioning properly and you therefore become *very* aware of them. In fact, you may hardly be able to think of anything else.

What is true of part of your person is true of all of it. If you are emotionally well and functioning optimally, you don't think about yourself for more than a fleeting moment. If you are conscious of yourself for a longer period of time, it is because, like your ears, eyes, or throat, there is an emotional aspect that is not completely well or is not functioning optimally.

When you are psychologically and emotionally healthy, you don't think about yourself. However, when an emotional problem vexes you, then your self-consciousness may push everything else out of your mind, and you may be totally focused on yourself.

If you are in severe physical pain, chances are that this occupies your attention so completely that you cannot focus competently on other matters, whether with regard to work or relating to other people. You may ask for time off from work or apologize to people because you cannot relate optimally to them. Much the same may happen when it is you *yourself* who is uncomfortable. *To the degree that you focus on yourself, to that degree you may be distracted from work or other people.* However, in contrast to physical pain, you may not even notice that you are being drawn to focus on yourself. Consequently, you may not even be aware that you are not functioning up to par. You may keep on working, but you are not at your best performance. You interact with people, but not as efficiently as you would like.

The *sifrei mussar* give great importance to *anivus* (humility). This is simply good mental health, and it enables you to function optimally.

STRENGTHENING ONE'S RESOLVE

In his chapter on *zerizus* (diligence, enthusiasm), Ramchal says that there are two matters that require *zerizus*. One is to have the impetus to start something, and second is to maintain the momentum to carry the project to completion. Not infrequently, a person may have great enthusiasm to embark on a project, but thereafter his enthusiasm may wane and he may abandon it. That is why one must maintain *zerizus*.

The Talmud says that although one should avoid the awesome responsibility of taking an oath, *tzaddikim* may vow to gird themselves against their *yetzer hara* (*Chagigah* 10a) and also to bind themselves to fulfilling mitzvos.

The Torah relates the battle of the four kings against the five, in which Abraham's nephew, Lot, was taken captive. Abraham did battle and defeated the four kings, rescuing his nephew.

The king of Sodom, in gratitude for Abraham's salvation, said, "Give me the people and take the possessions for yourself."

Abraham responded, "I lift up my hand to Hashem, G-d, the Most High, Maker of heaven and earth, if so much as a thread to a shoestring, or if I shall take anything of yours" (*Genesis* 14:1-23).

If Abraham did not want to take any of the spoils, why did he not simply say, "No, thank you"? Why did he have to take a solemn oath? The answer is that Abraham knew human nature, and knew that he, too, was vulnerable to the acquisitive drive. He might indeed feel determined not to take any of the possessions, but this determination might wane, and he might rationalize that he should take something after all, To protect himself against this, Abraham, at the moment that he felt that he should refuse to take anything, quickly took a solemn oath, thus making it impossible for him to retract from this decision.

If the great patriarch felt that he was at risk of losing his determination and changing his mind, how much more concerned should we be that we may lose our resolve! As Ramchal says, we should be alert to this tendency and guard ourselves against rationalizing to justify slackening our will to carry a project to its completion.

NOT AS BAD AS OTHERS

It has fallen to me to call the Jewish community's attention to problems they would prefer to believe do not exist among them: alcoholism, drug addiction, compulsive gambling, spouse abuse, Internet obscenity, increasing divorce rate. When I lecture about these, someone invariably points out that the incidence is not as great as it is in the general population. This is hardly a consolation, and it reminds me of a comment by my grandfather, the Kedushas Tzion of Bobov.

The prophet Malachi begins his prophesy with the words, "A burdensome prophesy by Malachi. 'I love you,' said Hashem, "And I said, 'Whereby do you love us?' 'Because Esau is a brother to Jacob. I loved Jacob and I hated Esau.'" My grandfather asked, "These appear to be very comforting and uplifting words, that Hashem loves us; why is this referred to as 'a burdensome prophesy'?"

He explained that Rebbe Levi Yitzchak of Berditchev cited the prayer the *Kohen Gadol* (High Priest) recited on Yom Kippur when he emerged from the Holy of Holies. "May Your people, Israel, not be dependent on one another nor on another nation." Rebbe Levi Yitzchak said that when a person, on his Judgment Day, is found to have many sins, his advocate angel will enter a defensive plea that he was less sinful than his neighbors; hence, he deserves mercy. But what happens in the case of the most sinful Jew, who is not better than any of his neighbors? The angel pleads, "He lived among heathens, who were worse than he"; hence, he deserves mercy.

Rebbe Levi Yitzchak said that the *Kohen Gadol* prayed that all Jews should be meritorious on their own account, and not be dependent for mercy on other Jews or on heathens.

That is why Malachi's prophesy was "burdensome." When he asked Hashem, "Whereby do You love us," and Hashem responded, "Jacob and Esau are brothers. I hate Esau because he is evil, and compared to Esau, Jacob is meritorious." If our only saving grace is that we are better than Esau, this is indeed a very sad and burdensome prophesy.

Similarly, any incidence of these improper behaviors is unacceptable. It is no consolation that we are not as bad as the general population. We must direct our efforts to prevent these behaviors and to treat them aggressively at their earliest occurrence. There should be zero tolerance for them.

SENSITIVITY TO FEELINGS

The Torah is very demanding about being considerate of people's feelings. "You shall not cause pain to any widow or orphan" (*Exodus* 22:21). Rashi says that this applies to every person, and that widows and orphans are mentioned only because since they are defenseless, people may not be careful not to cause them pain.

The Midrash cites two identical phrases in the Torah. When Esau learned that Jacob had received Isaac's blessings that were originally intended for Esau, "He cried a great and bitter cry" (*Genesis* 27:34). Similarly, when Mordechai became aware that Haman had issued a decree to annihilate all Jews, "He cried a great and bitter cry" (*Esther* 4:1). The Sages say that Haman's decree was partially due to Jacob having caused Esau grief. Think of it! The fact that Jacob receiving the blessing caused the evil Esau to suffer resulted in Jacob's children — all of Israel — to be in danger of being wiped out!

The *baalei mussar* ask why Jacob was being punished this way. After all, he was obliged to obey his mother's directive to impersonate Esau. He had no other option. They answer that when he saw how hurt Esau was, he nevertheless should have commiserated with him. Haman's decree was the consequence of Jacob's failure to feel Esau's pain. Even if what he did was proper, being indifferent to Esau's pain was a sin.

Sometimes circumstances demand that one act harshly. Whether it is a parent who must punish a child to discipline him, or on any occasion that one must do something that will result in someone's distress, one should not be insensitive to the other person's suffering. The Midrash describes how Hashem suffered when He allowed the Temple to be destroyed and Israel was sent into exile. In Hashem's system of justice, this was necessary, but He felt the pain of His children.

We interact with people many times each day. We must be cautious not to cause anyone to suffer.

MAKING A CHALLENGE "BITE SIZE"

"Jacob worked seven years for Rachel, and they seemed to him like just a few days because of his love for her" (*Genesis* 29:20). Some commentaries ask, "Is it not just the opposite? When someone is separated from a loved one, each day is an eternity. How could seven long years appear to him as just a few days?"

I am indebted to one of my recovering alcoholic patients for this insight. The only way an alcoholic can avoid drinking is by taking "one day at a time." If he were to think that he can never again drink alcohol, this knowledge would be so overwhelming that he would consider it impossible and he would not even try to abstain. Therefore, he is taught, "It is possible for you to abstain just this one day, isn't it? Then do so, and don't think about tomorrow. You will be able to deal with tomorrow's challenge tomorrow." By limiting the challenge to a single day, one can cope with it successfully.

Kerem Shlomo, commenting on *Psalms* 95:7, cites the verse, "If only you listen to Hashem's voice today," and says that the *yetzer hara* tells a person, "Why are you fighting a losing battle? You will never be able to withstand the deprivation of everything the Torah forbids. You might as well give up now." One's response to the *yetzer hara* should be, "I have to listen to Hashem's voice only today. I don't have to worry about the rest of my life. All I must do is just today."

My patient said that the word the Torah uses for "a few days" is *achadim*, which means "single days." If Jacob had considered that he must wait for Rachel seven years, it would not have been tolerable. Therefore, Jacob took the seven years as *yamim achadim*, single days, and as such, the seven years were manageable.

JACOB AND LABAN

The Midrash says that when Jacob left home to go to Haran, he detoured to the yeshivah of Shem and Eber, where he spent fourteen years. Why was this necessary? After all, he was constantly engaged in Torah study, as the Torah refers to him as "a dweller in tents" (*Genesis* 25:27) and the Midrash explains that this refers to the tents of Torah study. The answer is that Jacob knew how to live an authentic Torah life in the company of Isaac and Rebecca, but now he was going to be exposed to Laban and his corrupt environment, and he had to prepare himself so that he would remain true to Torah in that environment.

We may think that our children are safe because they grow up in our homes and in the yeshivos and Beis Yaakovs. But make no mistake about it. We live in an environment that is morally toxic, and we cannot prevent our children from being exposed to it. Like our ancestor Jacob, we must make great effort to help them resist the influence of the environment.

After spending years with Laban, Jacob said to Leah and Rachel, "I see your father's face, and it is not as it has been to me as in the past" (*Genesis* 31:5). This is generally taken to mean "Laban is no longer relating favorably to me." But one of the commentaries explains it differently. Jacob was saying, "In the past, when I looked at Laban, I was turned off by the evil in him. Now, I don't see the evil in him as clearly as it appeared in the past. If I have lost my aversion to evil, it is time that I leave here."

Our children learn proper *middos* by observing our reactions. If a fly falls into your soup, you discard the whole dish. Where did you learn that eating insects is disgusting? When you were a young child, and your mother saw you putting an insect in your mouth, she went into a near convulsion, shouting, "*Fui! Fui!*" accompanied by grimaces that left you with an indelible impression that eating insects is repugnant, and you retained that feeling for the rest of your life.. Had she calmly said, "Honey, bugs are not nice to eat," it is doubtful that it would have registered as effectively.

How do we react to an indecent picture in a newspaper or magazine? Do we have a gut reaction as to eating an insect? How do we react when we hear *lashon hara*? Do we put our hands over our ears and declare, "*Fui! Fui!* Poisonous talk." How do we react to violence? Our children are watching our reactions and are learning from them.

Jacob said, "The evil in Laban used to repel me. If I am becoming tolerant of it, I can no longer stay here." Our reactions to objectionable things should indicate that they are repulsive and that we have no tolerance whatsoever for them.

NOT ANGELS

I received the following query:

You've recommended that we inspire our children with stories about our gedolim. I wonder if that might not be counterproductive. These people were so angelic that our children might think, If that's what I must aspire to, I might as well give up now. That's unreachable. *Why aren't there more stories about mistakes they made, to show their human side?*

Here is my response:

I know of youngsters who love *chazzanus* and are taking voice lessons. When there is a concert featuring prominent *chazzanim*, their parents take them to hear the masters perform. The children might not aspire to become professional *chazzanim*, but that does not discourage them from improving their voices. They can understand that the performers were not born virtuosos, but became successful as a result of persistent effort. Many youngsters have thereby been motivated to practice longer and more often.

Our *gedolim* were not angels. They were great human beings, which puts them higher than angels. Angels were created holy, whereas the *gedolim* worked hard to become holy.

We should teach our children Torah *hashkafos*, and explain that by applying these, not only do we become better people, but things turn out better for us.

> While Rabbi YomTov Lipmann was the rabbi in a town in Europe, a woman brazenly insulted the Rebbetzin. The community leaders were outraged, and wished to penalize her. However, they could not take any action without the Rabbi's consent. Knowing that the Rabbi might dismiss the whole thing, they told the Rebbetzin to wait for the proper moment to inform her husband of the incident.
>
> On Friday night, when Rabbi YomTov was about to make *Kiddush*, the Rebbetzin stood at a distance. When he asked her what the problem was, she said, "I don't deserve to stand close to you. After all, this woman told me publicly how terrible a person I was."
>
> "When did this happen?" Rabbi YomTov asked.
>
> "On Wednesday," the Rebbetzin replied.
>
> "And you mean that you've been carrying a grudge for three whole days? The Torah says, 'Do not hate your fellow in your heart' [*Leviticus* 19:17]. Don't you say at the bedtime *Shema* that you forgive anyone who offended you? Come, let us go to this woman and ask her forgiveness for harboring a grudge against her."
>
> When they came to the woman's home, she was terrified that the Rabbi had come to pronounce a curse on her, and when the Rebbetzin said that she came to ask forgiveness for harboring a grudge, the woman burst into tears.
>
> "I'm the one who should be asking for forgiveness for being so rude." She embraced the Rebbetzin, and they wept on each other's shoulders.
>
> (from *Betzes HaShemesh BiGvuraso*, p. 148)

When R' Issar Zalman Meltzer was Rosh Yeshivah in Kletzk, he left for home one night, and a student, Moshe, accompanied the master. There had been a snowfall, and the unpaved streets were muddy. Planks of wood had been placed over the deeper mud puddles.

At one point, Moshe paused, "What is the problem?" R' Issar Zalman asked.

"Nothing, nothing," Moshe said.

R' Issar Zalman was adamant, "But something made you stop," he said.

"I took a pencil from my pocket and accidentally dropped it into the mud," he said.

"Was it a new or old pencil?" R' Issar Zalman asked.

"I bought it this week," Moshe said.

"Then it is new and we must find it," R' Issar Zalman said, and began groping in the mud.

When they could not find the pencil, R' Issar Zalman continued home and told his wife, "Please give me the lantern. Moshe accompanied me home, and as a result he lost his pencil. I must help him find it."

The Rebbetzin protested. She would not allow him to go out in the cold of night to look for a pencil! Moshe and others who were present joined to discourage R' Issar Zalman, who persisted, "I know that Moshe is upset that he lost the pencil, and I am obligated to help him find it."

Only with great effort and tearful pleas by Moshe did they succeed in convincing the master not to go out again!

That is a sense of responsibility.

(from *BeDerech Etz HaChaim*, p. 276)

Angels? No. Just great human beings. And if we adopt *middos* similar to these, we can inspire our children, who know that we are indeed very human, but we aspire to Torah *middos*.

ALL SINS ARE THEFT

Rambam says that confessing one's sins is an integral element of *teshuvah* (*Teshuvah* 5:7). The source for this is the verse, "They shall confess their sins" (*Numbers* 5:7). This verse refers to one who has committed theft and swore falsely that he did not do so. The *Chidushei HaRim*, R' Yitzchak Meir of Gur, asks, "Inasmuch as there are 365 prohibitions in the Torah, why did the Torah choose to specify the need to confess one's sins in regard to theft?"

R' Yitzchak Meir explains that if a person borrows an item for a specific use, he is not permitted to use it for any purpose other that that specified; if he does, it constitutes theft, because he is using someone's property without permission.

Hashem has provided us with numerous abilities so that we can accomplish so many things. He has given us the ability to speak so that we may pray, study Torah, and communicate properly. He has given us the means to hear so that we may hear the words of Torah and receive proper communication. He has given us vision so that we may see the words of Torah, the beauty of creation, and be able to do the things necessary to sustain life. So it is with all parts of our body and with all our abilities. These were given for a specific purpose.

If we use our ability to speak to say *lashon hara* or untruths, if we look at indecent things, or if we use any of our skills in a way that transgresses Torah, we are using the faculties that Hashem gave us for purposes other than those specified — and that constitutes theft. Thus, every sin is committing theft, and that is why the need to confess one's sins was stated in regard to theft.

We pride ourselves on being honest, and we would never think of taking something that does not belong to us. Let us remember that any transgression of Torah, even if one does not consider it to be a major sin, is nevertheless a serious sin of theft.

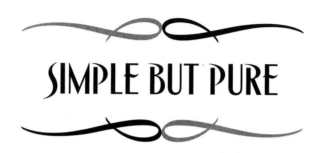

SIMPLE BUT PURE

There are many esoteric, kabbalistic thoughts (*kavannos*) one may have when performing mitzvos, and they are known only to those select few who have been initiated into the mysteries of kabbalah.

Before Rosh Hashanah, Rebbe Levi Yitzchak of Berditchev stated that he wanted to interview candidates to blow the shofar. Several people volunteered, and R' Levi Yitzchak tested their knowledge of the kabbalistic *kavannos*.

At the end, one man asked to be interviewed. He was a devout but rather unlearned person, and R' Levi Yitzchak was surprised that this person might be privy to kabbalistic secrets. Perhaps he was one of the hidden *tzaddikim* who concealed his true identity, the Rebbe thought.

"What are the *kavannos* for blowing the shofar?" Rebbe Levi Yitzchak asked.

The man began to cry. "Rebbe," he said, "I have a daughter of marriageable age, but I will not be able to find a *shidduch* for her because I do not have a dowry. My *kavannos* are, '*Ribono shel Olam* [Master of the universe], I am fulfilling Your will by blowing the shofar as You commanded. Please, grant my wish that I can provide my daughter with a dowry so that she can be married.'"

Rebbe Levi Yitzchak was touched. "Your *kavannos* are the finest of all! You will blow the shofar for us!"

THE WORLD AS A MIRROR

Hashem said to Cain, "Surely, if you improve yourself, you will be forgiven. But if you do not improve yourself, sin rests at the door" (*Genesis* 4:7).

R' Shneur Zalman of Liadi, author of *Tanya*, said that the Hebrew words lend themselves to an additional interpretation. "If you improve yourself, and develop desirable character traits, you will be able to tolerate everyone. If you do not improve yourself and you will be sinful, you will find sin everywhere."

Psychology speaks of the defense mechanism, *projection*, which means that you project your own faults or ideas onto others.

This concept can be found in the Talmud, written some 2000 years ago: "A person disqualifies others with his own faults." If a person calls others illegitimate, he should be investigated, because it is likely that he himself is illegitimate.

The Baal Shem Tov took this one step further. He said, "The world is a mirror." Inasmuch as a person is generally blind to his own character defects, he is shown them in other people. Hence, when you notice a fault in someone else, do a careful soul-searching, because you probably have the faults that you see in others.

One might argue, "I happened to see someone doing something wrong. Why does that mean that I am guilty of that wrong?"

Here is a simple experiment. Have ten people stand at a busy street corner for several minutes, and then ask them to report what they saw. Although they all observed the identical scene, they will relate different things. What caused each person to notice the things he reported? Nothing just "happens." Something attracted the attention of one person but did not attract the attention of another. There may be a variety of subconscious factors that account for the selectivity of their perception.

The Baal Shem Tov said that if a person did not harbor at least a smattering of a particular personality defect, his attention would not have been drawn to see it in another person.

R' Shneur Zalman said, "To the degree that you are free of character defects, to that degree you will be able to tolerate others, because you will not see them as undesirable. If you are sinful, you will see sin wherever you look."

We would be able to have vast self-improvement if we searched within ourselves for the character defects we so easily see in others.

This is an excellent way to attain self-awareness, but we must be courageous enough to admit it to ourselves.

JOY WITH TREMORS

"Serve Hashem with awe that you may rejoice when there is trembling" (*Psalms* 2:11).

This appears to be a bit inconsistent. Joy does usually not accompany awe and tremors.

A chassid once came to the Alter Rebbe (Rebbe Shneur Zalman of Liadi, author of *Tanya*), and presented him with a *kvittel* (petition) in which he enumerated his many needs. The Alter Rebbe studied the *kvittel* and said, "It seems that you have given much thought to your needs. Have you also given much thought to why you are needed?"

The chassid was shaken by this reprimand. He had been concentrating on his needs, but had not given too much thought to whether he was accomplishing the purpose for which he had been created.

Yet this sharp reprimand was uplifting. There is no depression worse than feeling worthless, that one serves no purpose. Being reminded that he was needed, that there was a special mission for which Hashem created him, was exhilarating.

The *sefarim* tell us that Hashem waits for our prayers and takes great pleasure in our mitzvos. The psalmist says, "Fortunate is the man who fears Hashem, who greatly desires His mitzvos" (*Psalms* 112:1). One of the Chassidic masters said that the verse can also be read as "Fortunate is the man who fears Hashem. He [Hashem] greatly desires his mitzvos." I.e., Hashem has great desire for the mitzvos of those who fear Him.

Thus, there can be joy amid tremors. Tremors of awe — and joy in knowing how important one is to Hashem, and that one's life has meaning. Perhaps this was what the psalmist refers to when he writes, "Serve Hashem with awe that you may rejoice when there is trembling" (*Psalms* 2:11).

WHAT'S MAJOR AND WHAT'S MINOR?

When R' Aryeh Leib, author of *Shaagas Aryeh,* became Rav of Metz, he was displeased that on Shavuos, the liturgical poem *Akdamus* was read after the *Kohen* recited the *berachah* on the Torah reading, and decreed that it should be read *before* the *berachah.* Some of the townspeople were annoyed that he insisted on changing their custom,

R' Aryeh Leib was advised that a newly appointed rav has the privilege to write an entry in the shul *pinkus* (chronicles). He then inscribed into the *pinkus* the Ten Commandments, and explained, "I see that the people are very meticulous in observing the shul's customs, even though these may not have any basis in halachah. However, they do not seem to be as scrupulous in observing the Ten Commandments. I, therefore, wrote the Ten Commandments into the shul's *pinkus,* in the hope that they will give these the same consideration they give to customs."

R' Aryeh Leib's observation is relevant today. There are people who will insist on preserving some traditions, although these may not have any halachic basis, while neglecting major Torah requirements.

> It is related that a man was angry at the proprietor of a Judaica store for refusing to open the store on Shabbos so that the man could obtain a copy of the *Shir HaMaalos* (the traditional *shemirah* [protective psalm]) for his newborn child. The *shemirah* was important to him, but Shabbos was not.

We must be careful to judge what is truly important.

TRUE AHAVAS YISRAEL (LOVE OF ONE'S FELLOW JEW)

T he following incidents emphasize the importance of true *ahavas yisrael*, love of one's fellow Jew.

R' Baruch Teumim-Frankel once saw that his daughter and one of the household help were joking and laughing, and he said to them, "Don't you know that Mordechai, the proprietor of the bathhouse, is seriously ill? How can you be so light headed, joking and laughing, when someone in your community is suffering?"

A very wealthy woman wanted to arrange a *shidduch* between her son and a daughter of R' Baruch Teumim-Frankel. When she came to the Rav's home, she found him despondent.

"Is there anything wrong?" she asked.

The Rav told her that one of the children in town was very ill.

"And that's why you are despondent?" she questioned in surprise.

The Rav asked her to leave, because he was not interested in a *shidduch* with a family that can be indifferent to a person's suffering.

R' Yitzchak of Vorki cited the Talmudic statement of R' Z'eira, whose students asked him the secret of his longevity.

R' Z'eira replied, "I never was glad at someone's distress."

Why does R' Z'eira consider that trait to be a virtue? It would seem that to gloat at someone's distress would be abominable. R' Yitzchak explained that R' Z'eira meant that if there were occasions that gave him personal joy, he never was able to feel happy if he was aware that there was someone who was suffering.

R' Elimelech of Lizhensk took upon himself two years of wandering in exile to atone for his "sins." Upon his return to Lizhensk, one of the townsfolk informed him that his son, Eliezer, was very ill.

R' Elimelech rushed home, and asked his wife, "What happened to Eliezer?"

The wife said, "Nothing has happened to Eliezer. He is in *cheder*."

R' Elimelech said, "But someone told me that Eliezer was very sick."

The wife though a moment and said, "Oh, he was referring to one of the neighbors, whose child, Eliezer, is sick."

R' Elimelech was momentarily relieved, then said to himself, *So, Melech, after two years of exile you feel a difference between your Eliezer and another person's Eliezer? Then you have accomplished nothing with your exile.*

Whereupon he turned around and went into exile for another year.

These are just a few examples of true *ahavas Yisrael*.

PSYCHOLOGICAL BLINDNESS

Although the following essay was included in *Twerski on Chumash*, I believe it is important enough to bear repeating.

A psychological phenomenon known as *denial* indicates that a person is unable to see something that is obvious, and this inability is as real as physical blindness. No amount of coaxing will enable a blind person to see a rainbow. In prohibiting a judge from taking a bribe, the Torah says that a bribe "blinds" the judge, who is thereupon unable to see anything averse to the litigant who bribed him.

In the narrative of Joseph and his brothers (*Genesis* Chs. 37-45), the Torah states that the brothers did not recognize Joseph because at 17 his beard had not yet grown, but now he was bearded. However, Rashi says that Joseph bore a strong resemblance to Jacob, who was bearded, so there should have been an obvious similarity to Jacob's appearance, specifically now that Joseph had a beard.

The Midrash states that when Joseph ordered Shimon to be taken hostage, Shimon fought the soldiers, and they could not subdue him. Joseph then sent his son Menashe, who gave Shimon one blow, causing him to fall. Shimon then declared, "This blow must be from one of my father's household." How could anyone in Egypt be of Jacob's household unless it was a child of Joseph?

When Joseph hosted the brothers at dinner, he seated them according to their seniority. Rashi says that Joseph said, "Reuben, Simeon, Levi, Yehudah, etc, children of one mother, sit here. Dan, Naftali, children of one mother, sit here." The brothers were bewildered. How could he possibly have this knowledge?

When you put all these facts together, it is incomprehensible that they did not suspect that this was Joseph. The explanation is that they were so determined not to believe the validity of Joseph's dreams, virtually brainwashed by this, that they were rendered psychologically blind and could not see the obvious.

This narrative conveys an extremely important teaching. We are all "bribed" by our own interests. We may be unable to see what should be evident.

It is classic that the life of an alcoholic may be falling apart, shattered in every way by his drinking, and everyone is pointing this out to him. However, his addiction to alcohol renders him blind to the obvious.

There have been instances in which parents have begged their child not to marry the person with whom he/she has become infatuated, because that person is of very poor character, but the young man/woman is blinded by passion. When the infatuation fades, he/she discovers that their parents' objections were valid.

How can we avoid errors in judgment due to our being blinded by our own interests? Only by seeking the opinion and counsel of others who are objective and can see what we cannot. Availing ourselves of the appropriate objective observer can prevent great harm.

CONCEPTS OF TZEDAKAH

R' Chaim Halberstam, the *Tzaddik* of Sanz, was lavish in giving *tzedakah*. In Europe there was no welfare system, and the poor often lacked even the barest necessities. The *Tzaddik* said, "I learned to give *tzedakah* from R' Hirsch of Rimanov. However, I could not match his nature. When R' Hirsch had given away everything he had, he was at peace, but when I have nothing more to give and I know that there are still needy poor, my heart aches."

One time the *Tzaddik* was asked, "The *Shulchan Aruch* states that there is a limitation; one should not give more than 20 percent of one's assets for *tzedakah*. Why does the Rebbe violate this and give away everything he has?"

The *Tzaddik* answered, "You do not understand the *Shulchan Aruch*, which is referring to how one should fulfill the mitzvah of *tzedakah*. Every mitzvah has a *shiur*, a specified amount to fulfill that mitzvah. For example, the mitzvah of matzah on Pesach is to eat a *kezayis* [the volume of an olive]. For the mitzvah of shofar, there are a designated number of sounds to blow. So, for the mitzvah of *tzedakah*, the limit is 20 percent.

"But there is another aspect to *tzedakah,* over and above its being a mitzvah. With *tzedakah* one can attain forgiveness for one's sins. Just as a person would give away everything he owns to be cured from an illness, so he can give away everything to remove his sins."

THE PIVOTAL ROLE OF SELF-ESTEEM

My preoccupation with the theme of self-esteem has been vindicated by the contemporary ethicist, Rabbi Shlomo Wolbe, in his work, *Alei Shur* Vol. 1, in which he makes the bold statement that self-awareness and self-esteem are cornerstones of Torah observance. Rabbi Wolbe says that there is a prevailing attitude that the study of *mussar* is depressing because it requires a thorough soul-searching to uncover one's character defects. A person who concentrates primarily on finding his faults is indeed prone to becoming depressed, and may even feel that his effort to achieve spirituality is futile.

R' Wolbe writes that this occurs only if we study *mussar* improperly. Before Hashem gave the Torah to Israel, He said, "You shall be to

Me the most beloved treasure of all peoples ... a kingdom of ministers and a holy nation" (*Exodus* 19:5-6). After the giving of the Torah, Moses said to the Israelites, "[Hashem spoke to you] to elevate you ... so that you shall not sin" (ibid. 20:17). The prerequisite for receiving the Torah was for the Israelites to appreciate their lofty status, and the formula for observing the Torah was to be aware of their superior spiritual status.

The prerequisite of *mussar* is to be aware of one's importance. "A person *is obligated* to say, 'The world was created for me'" (*Sanhedrin* 37a). A person must be aware of his uniqueness; he must know that in this world there is a specific task that only he can accomplish. No one else, from the time of Abraham until the end of time, even all together, can fulfill what Hashem has designated as one particular person's unique mission in the universe.

Learning *mussar* this way is uplifting, anything but depressing.

If a person is wearing soiled work clothes, he is not careful to avoid staining them further. What difference does one more stain make? However, if one is wearing a fine, expensive silk garment, he is most cautious to avoid it being stained, and if a stain should occur, he will quickly seek to remove it without damaging the garment.

A person must realize how special and precious he or she is, to be the bearer of a Divine *neshamah*, which is part of Hashem Himself. Only after appreciating one's inherent greatness and importance can one proceed to remove the "stains" on one's character.

Awareness of one's uniqueness and special mission in the world gives one a feeling of self-esteem, which is far removed from *gaavah* (vanity; arrogance). It is this very feeling of importance that makes one realize how much he must do to fulfill his mission, and this can give him the feeling of *anivus* (humility), the polar opposite of *gaavah*.

HASHEM'S FORGIVENESS

One Yom Kippur, in order to impress the worshipers with Hashem's forgiveness, a rabbi held his sweet, curly-haired, 3-year-old daughter in his arms and said, "Is there anything she would do for which I would not forgive her?"

This was indeed a powerful message. The Baal Shem Tov said, "I wish I could have the love for the greatest *tzaddik* that Hashem has for the worst *rasha* [sinner]." Hashem's love for us is far greater than the love of a father for his beautiful child.

Yet, if the darling little girl wanted a cookie before supper, the parents would refuse to give it to her, and if she helped herself to the cookie jar after Mommy said, "No," they would reprimand her, and if necessary, punish her. They would do so because not only will the cookie before supper ruin her appetite and interfere with her nutrition, she must learn to listen to her parents. This would be done out of love for the child, to maximize her nutrition and health, although at age 3, the child cannot understand this.

Relative to Hashem's infinite wisdom, our intellect is less than juvenile. We cannot begin to grasp His infinite wisdom, but we must accept on faith that as a loving father, whatever He does is for our own welfare.

Admittedly, this requires great faith and can be a severe test. How can a tornado or a tsunami be to anyone's benefit? Why do so many innocent people endure hardship and suffering? Moses posed this question to Hashem, and Hashem told him that as long as he inhabits a human body, he cannot grasp Hashem's ways.

> R' Shimon of Yaraslav lived to be over 100. When asked for the secret of his longevity, he said, "When people challenge Hashem and want an explanation, Hashem says, 'Come up here, and I'll tell you.' I don't question Hashem, so He does not invite me to join him."

Insofar as forgiveness is concerned, the rabbi mentioned in the opening paragraph is correct. The only caveat is that we must acknowledge that we did wrong, ask for forgiveness, and commit ourselves not to repeat the sin. If we do so, we should be aware that Hashem's love for us is so great that there is nothing we could do for which He would not forgive us.

JUSTICE WITH CHESED

We close the prayers of *Avinu Malkeinu* with "do with us *tzedakah vachesed*," which is usually translated as "charity and kindness." However, *tzedakah* is not charity. *Tzedek* means "justice." Kindness must be accompanied by justice.

> The wife of R' Zusia of Anipole had ordered a dress to be sewn for her. When the dress was ready, she came to the tailor's shop. She noticed that he sighed heavily as he presented her with the finished garment. She asked why he was sad. He replied that his daughter was soon to be married, and when she had seen her father sewing this dress, she was thrilled, assuming he was making it for her. When he told his daughter that the dress was for a customer and that he could not afford to make her a dress, she broke down crying.

R' Zusia's wife took pity on the young bride and told the tailor, "Give the dress to your daughter. My husband will not complain if I do not have a new dress."

When his wife told R' Zusia that she had given the dress to the young woman, R' Zusia praised her highly, saying that she had done a great mitzvah.

"Did you pay the tailor for his work?" R' Zusia then asked.

"Pay him? Why, I let him keep my dress. Isn't that enough?"

R' Zusia shook his head. "You commissioned him to sew a dress, and he earned his wage for that. You could have kept the dress for yourself. The fact that you decided to do a mitzvah and give your dress to his daughter is indeed praiseworthy, but that does not exempt you from paying the tailor for the work he did for you."

That is what is meant by *tzedakah vachesed*. Kindness must be accompanied by justice. You cannot do a kindness on someone else's account.

THE ULTIMATE IN HYPOCRISY

A bove, in "Kosher Money," I pointed out that some people have grossly distorted ideas about *Yiddishkeit*. I cannot think of an example of such distorted values as that of a story related to me by a friend.

The Chofetz Chaim was extremely scrupulous in his honesty. Before selling any *sefer*, he would laboriously go through the *sefer* page by page to make certain that there were no missing or defective pages. This consumed many hours of his time. Inasmuch as the Chofetz Chaim never allowed even a single moment to be diverted from Torah study, spending so much time carefully checking his *sefarim* was obviously because he considered selling a defective *sefer* to be a greater sin than *bittul* Torah.

When he finished checking a *sefer*, the Chofetz Chaim would write the word *mugah* (free of error) on the frontispiece to indicate that the *sefer* was complete and not defective.

My friend had a volume of *Mishnah Berurah* that bore the Chofetz Chaim's note, *mugah*, and he greatly valued having a *sefer* with an inscription in the Chofetz Chaim's handwriting. One day he was shocked to discover that this page was missing. Obviously, a visitor who had noticed it wished to avail himself of the Chofetz Chaim's handwriting and had torn out the page!

Can there be a greater sacrilege? This man's respect for the Chofetz Chaim was so great that he violated everything the Chofetz Chaim stood for, committing the sin of stealing someone else's property in order to have the Chofetz Chaim's handwriting!

We must be careful to keep our priorities straight.

EMPATHY

Only an authoritative *posek* may determine when and if the halachic rulings of the *Shulchan Aruch* may be waived. *Yoreh Deah* states that a mourner (i.e., one within the year following death of a parent) should not serve as *shaliach tzibbur* (leader of services) on festivals or on the High Holy Days.

> The regular *shaliach tzibbur* in the shul of R' Yosef Chaim Sonnenfeld in Jerusalem passed away two weeks before Rosh Hashanah, and the *kehillah* (congregation) needed someone to serve this function. R' Yosef Chaim Sonnenfeld told them that there was no need to look for a replacement. The congregants assumed that R' Yosef Chaim was planning to lead the services himself.
>
> On Rosh Hashanah eve, R' Yosef Chaim Sonnenfeld told the son of the late *shaliach tzibbur* to lead the services. All those in shul were

astonished, because Rosh Hashanah came out within the *sheloshim* (30-day period of mourning) of the young man's father's death.

R' Yosef Chaim Sonnenfeld said, "The practice that a mourner does not lead the services is because of *kavod hatzibbur* [the respect for the congregation]. For many years, the wife of the *shaliach tzibbur* has listened to her husband lead the services. His recent death is a fresh wound. Can you imagine the intensity of her grief when she will hear someone else replacing her husband as *shaliach tzibbur*?

"The son's voice is similar to his late father's. When she hears her son's voice, knowing that he is assuming his father's position will bring her some comfort. Can there be anything more desirable to the *kehillah* than gladdening the heart of a widow, which is so great a mitzvah?"

(from *Ha'ish al HaChomah* 2:13)

ADD TO YOUR MITZVOS

"If a person did not commit an *aveirah* [sin], he receives reward as if he had done a mitzvah. That is, if the opportunity to commit an *aveirah* presented itself" (*Kiddushin* 39b).

Many authorities believe that in doing a mitzvah one must have *kavannah* (intent) to do a mitzvah. It follows that in abstaining from an *aveirah*, one must have *kavannah* that he is doing so to fulfill the will of Hashem.

Suppose you are hungry and happen to pass a McDonald's. You should think, *I am abstaining from eating* tereifah *because Hashem forbids it.*

> In a town near Pressburg, a wealthy man's investments failed and he lost everything. He came to the Chasam Sofer, crying about his bitter plight. "I believe I could start anew if I had the means to do it, but no one will lend me the money."

"How much do you need?" the Chasam Sofer asked. The man stated a considerable amount. The Chasam Sofer went to his breakfront and took out several silver items. "Go sell these and use the money to start a new business, and Hashem should bless you with *hatzlachah* [success]."

The man did as he was told, and eventually his business prospered. He then came to the Chasam Sofer to express his gratitude and return the value of the silver. He then said, "I have a special gift for the Rav," handing the Chasam Sofer a little box. The Chasam Sofer opened the box, and found a beautiful diamond.

The Chasam Sofer said, "This is indeed a beautiful diamond." He then took it to the window and kept marveling at its beauty. Several of his students were present, and he showed the diamond to them so that they could likewise admire its beauty. Then he said to the man, "I cannot accept this diamond from you, because that would be violating the Torah prohibition of accepting *ribbis* [interest on a loan]," and he returned the diamond.

The Chasam Sofer then addressed his students. "A person doing business borrows and lends money and has many opportunities to fulfill the mitzvah of not giving or taking *ribbis*. But when do I have such an opportunity? That is why I praised the beauty of the diamond. It provided me with the opportunity to fulfill the mitzvah of not accepting *ribbis*."

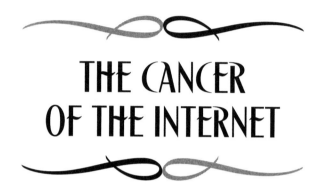

THE CANCER OF THE INTERNET

Not a week goes by that I don't get several calls about new casualties to the Internet. Some people call in desperation about themselves, feeling trapped into a behavior from which they have unsuccessfully tried to extricate themselves. Others, equally desperate, call about a family member. *There is no immunity.* The general public would be shocked to learn the caliber of some of the people who have fallen prey to this problem.

While restricting access to the Internet would appear to be a logical solution, it is simply not realistic. The use of Internet, even just for business needs, is widespread. Filters can be effective to prevent accidental exposure to improper scenes, and can be helpful for people who sincerely want to stop. But the Satan has become overpowering and is claiming victims, destroying spiritual lives, marriages, and families.

When the swine flu epidemic was at its height, a man told me that he was traveling by car to a city 600 miles away. Why? Because he was in close contact with his infant grandchildren and was afraid of exposure to a carrier of the swine flu virus at the airport or on a plane. The awareness of the gravity of the problem and the possible consequences warranted his driving ten hours! This man had no false illusions about immunity. Even if we are secure about ourselves, we should be seriously concerned about our children. The technology is advancing every day. There is no safe place to hide out.

What can we do? One phrase comes to mind, that of the patriarch Abraham to Abimelech, "There is just no fear of G-d in this place" (*Genesis* 20:11). Whatever else one may do, if there is no *yiras Shamayim* (awe of Hashem), everything is possible, even the most immoral behavior.

But don't we have strong *yiras Shamayim*? *Baruch Hashem*, we have wonderful yeshivos and seminaries. We have *glatt* kosher meat, *chalav yisrael, pas Yisrael,* and *kemach yashan.*

But listen to the Talmud:

> When Rabban Yochanan ben Zakkai was in his last days, his *talmidim* asked for his *berachah*. He said, "May your fear of Hashem be as great as your fear of people."
>
> His *talmidim* were shocked. "Is that what you think of us?"
>
> Rabban Yochanan said, "*Halevai* you would achieve that! When a person does an *aveirah* he is concerned that no person should see him. It does not bother him that Hashem sees him" (*Berachos* 25b).

Just think of it! The students of Rabban Yochanan ben Zakkai! People whose greatness in Torah and holiness is beyond what we can imagine, yet he felt that they might be lacking in fear of Hashem. How can we say about ourselves that we have adequate fear of Hashem? Remember what *Chovos HaLevavos* says, "You may be asleep, but the *yetzer hara* is awake." Awake and unrelenting.

What can we do to increase *yiras Shamayim*? Rashi provides the answer." To observe those easy mitzvos that we tend to trample upon" (*Deuteronomy* 7:12). *Baruch Hashem*, we do not trample on kashrus, on Shabbos, or on *chametz* on Pesach, but unfortunately, we may trample on *middos: ka'as* (anger), *lashon hara, kinah* (jealousy), *sinah* (hatred), *ga'avah* (arrogance), *shekker* (lying). We should keep before us the words of Rebbe Chaim Vital, that we should take even greater precaution with *middos* than we do with *aveiros*! *Middos* are the key to *yiras Shamayim*. *Middos* give the person a sense of holiness and dignity so that he would not allow himself to be soiled with the *tumah* (impurity) of the Internet.

Let us be honest with ourselves. Do we sometimes lose our temper? The Talmud says that this is equivalent to *avodah zarah* (idolatry). Do we sometimes listen to or speak *lashon hara*, which is equivalent to the three cardinal sins of *avodah zarah, shefichas damim* (bloodshed), and *arayos* (illicit relations)? Do we sometimes deviate from the truth? No number of *chumros* (stringencies) can be considered *yiras Shamayim* if we are not meticulously careful about *middos*.

It is easy to buy kosher food. It is *not* easy to become master of our *middos*. It may be the most difficult challenge of our lives. But think of the person who will drive ten hours for fear that he may be exposed to the swine flu virus and how disastrous this can be to his grandchildren. If our homes do not become fortresses of *true yiras Shamayim*, our children are at risk of being infected by the virus of the Internet. Remember the words of the patriarch Abraham, "There is just no fear of G-d in this place." Without true *yiras Shamayim*, nothing else will be effective.

GUARD YOUR TONGUE

The Chofetz Chaim was at an inn, and ate together with a Rav. When the innkeeper asked if they were satisfied with the food, the Chofetz Chaim said, "The food was excellent."

The Rav said, "It was quite good, but it was missing salt."

The Chofetz Chaim said to the Rav, "Do you realize what you have done with your comment? The innkeeper will scold the cook, who is probably a poor widow who needs the job, and he may dismiss her. You have spoken *lashon hara* by saying that she did not cook well, and you caused me and the innkeeper to listen to *lashon hara*. She will swear that she had tasted the food and that it was seasoned properly, so you will have caused her to swear falsely."

The Rav said, "With all due respect, you are greatly exaggerating an innocent comment I made."

The Chofetz Chaim said, "Let's go into the kitchen." They did so, and found the cook in tears because the innkeeper was rebuking her and threatening to dismiss her.

The Rav apologized to the cook, and the Chofetz Chaim prevailed on the innkeeper not to dismiss her.

The Chofetz Chaim said, "See how much thought a person must give to what seems to be an innocent comment."

The Talmud says that *lashon hara* can destroy three people: the one who speaks it, the one who hears it, and the person about whom one spoke. While physical harm can be effected only when the victim is in proximity of the assailant, defamatory speech has the capacity to destroy someone who is thousands of miles away.

Hashem created the entire universe through ten utterances. Words can create worlds, and words can destroy them.

THE TOXICITY OF RAGE

In several essays, I have pointed out that there are three phases to anger: 1. the *feeling* upon being provoked; 2. the *reaction* to the provocation (rage); 3. the *retention* of the feeling (resentment). Whereas 2 and 3 are controllable, one has little or no control over the first phase. When the Talmud condemns *ka'as* (anger) (*Nedarim* 22a), it is referring to the *rage* reaction, not to the initial feeling.

The Midrash states that on three occasions Moses became angry, and each time erred; the Midrash concludes that anger will cause a wise person to lose his wisdom and a prophet to lose his prophecy (*Vayikra Rabbah* 13). R' Chaim Shmulevitz says that these are not punishments, but natural consequences of rage, and occur even if the rage was justified. If someone is justified to reach for something in a flame, his hand will be burned, not as a punishment, but as a natural consequence (*Sichos Mussar* 5733:23)

When a typhus epidemic broke out, R' Yisrael of Salant instructed the yeshivah students to care for the sick, and on Shabbos, to do whatever is necessary for the ailing person, regardless of what it involves, because all the restrictions of work on Shabbos are suspended in the event of *pikuach nefesh*.

The father of a student who had been cared for by other students thanked R' Yisrael for assigning the students to care for those stricken by the disease, but added, "I do think that the boys were lax in the observance of Shabbos, because they did things that were not absolutely essential for the patient."

R' Yisrael raised his voice and shouted at the man. "You have the chutzpah to tell me about the halachos of Shabbos? These boys' parents entrusted their children to me, and I am responsible for their lives." The man promptly apologized.

R' Yisrael explained that the reason he shouted was because there were several students present when the man made his comment, and had he not reacted vigorously, these students might have curtailed their actions in caring for the ill. Although he was fully justified in reacting with rage, and it was a calculated action rather than an emotional reaction, R' Yisrael never forgot the incident and did *teshuvah* for it all his life.

Many people lose their temper when things do not go their way or when they are provoked to anger. As Rav Shmulevitz points out, this is self-destructive even when justified. How careful we should be to avoid rage!

TEXTING TO HASHEM

One morning at Shacharis, a man had his *tallis* and *tefillin* ready to don, but instead of putting them on, he was texting a message. This irritated another worshiper. "For heaven's sake," he grumbled aloud. "You came to shul to *daven*, and you'll be out in thirty minutes. What is so important that it can't wait until after *davening*? Or were you texting to Hashem?"

The phrase, "texting to Hashem," caught my attention. I began to reflect, *What is unique about texting?* and it occurred to me that a message that would normally be written, "How are you? Would you be able to send me the data before tomorrow evening? I'll be away after that," would probably come out in a much shorter text message as, "How R U? Wud U B abl 2 send data B4 2morrow PM? I'll B away aftr."

During Shacharis, I saw the people *davening* at a pace with which

Texting to Hashem / 153

I could not keep up, and I wondered, *Are they perhaps texting to Hashem, condensing and abbreviating the tefillos?*

Texting may get the message across, and this may indeed be the bottom line of some communications. However, the tone of the message may be forfeited. In prayer, the tone is as important as the content. We pray, *shema koleinu*, listen to *our voice*. "The Children of Israel groaned because of the work and they cried out. Their outcry because of the work went up to Hashem" (*Exodus* 2:23). "You hear the sound of the shofar" (Rosh Hashanah prayers). Sometimes it is the sound, the *krechtz* (sigh), that is the message. A textinglike prayer surely deletes this aspect and misses the point.

On the other hand, perhaps texting to Hashem is not such a bad idea after all. Voice digitalization was heralded as a major technological marvel. Ha! We had that 3000 years ago. At Sinai, "The entire people saw the sounds," and Rashi comments, "They saw what is usually heard" (*Exodus* 20:15). How right King Solomon was, "There is nothing new beneath the sun" (*Ecclesiastes* 1:9).

There is obviously something special about the written word. Our prayers on Rosh Hashanah and Yom Kippur are replete with requests for the written word. "Remember us for life ... and *inscribe us* in the Book of Life .... Our Father, our King, *inscribe us* in the book of redemption and salvation, etc."

"Then those who fear Hashem spoke to one another, and Hashem listened and heard, and *a book of remembrance* was written before Him" (*Ethics of the Fathers* 3:3). The Talmud then states that it is meritorious not only if two people study Torah together, but even if a person studies Torah alone. However, there is an advantage if two people study Torah together, because *then it is written in the book of remembrance.*

Hashem's memory is perfect. What need is there for things to be written down?

Perhaps this is because the Rosh Hashanah – Yom Kippur prayer, *Nesaneh Tokef,* states that on Judgment Day, the book of remembrance is opened and what is written there is read, *and the seal of every person's hand is in it.*

The recording of everything is because there is no need for any external testimony. Everything we say or do is digitalized and transcribed, and our own signature is set to it. We ourselves testify to what we say and do.

Perhaps there is some merit in the concept of "texting to Hashem." If we really think about it, we may refine our behavior.

POOR BUT WORTHY

The Talmud cites an example of "poor but worthy." The poor brought their *bikkurim* (offering of first-ripened fruits) to the Temple in woven baskets, and the wealthy brought them in gold and silver vessels. The woven baskets were retained in the Temple, while the gold and silver vessels were returned to their owners (*Bava Kamma* 92a).

"But what was the reason for this?" asked the Chassidic master, Rebbe David of Tolna.

> The Rebbe explained that he had once notified the inhabitants of a village that he was coming for Shabbos. When the word reached town, many people were jubilant, but not all. Chaim, the tailor, came home glowing with joy. "The Rebbe is coming for Shabbos!" he said. But then he became gloomy.

"What's wrong?" his wife asked.

"The Rebbe collects money for *tzedakah*, and I have nothing to give him," Chaim said sadly.

His wife said, "Don't you let that bother you. I will do some extra baking and sell it, and we'll put together a ruble for *tzedakah*."

That same day, Yona, the town's wealthiest citizen, glumly returned home from shul.

"What happened?" his wife asked.

"Oh," Yona answered, "the Rebbe is coming to town."

"So why are you so glum?" she asked. "You should be happy."

"Well," Yona said, "the Rebbe solicits funds to help marry off poor *kallahs*, and he will put the touch on me. That will cost me at least another fifty rubles."

Rebbe David said, "To me, Chaim's single ruble is dearer than Yona's fifty rubles." He continued. "Something similar occurred regarding *bikkurim*."

The poor person had just a few fruit trees, and one day he was elated, saying to his wife, "I just noticed some fruits ripening. I'll be able to take them to Jerusalem to the Temple." But then he became sad.

"What happened that you are sad?" his wife asked.

"I need some kind of container for the *bikkurim*, but we don't have anything decent."

The wife said, "That's no problem. Our daughter and I will weave a basket for you that will be beautiful."

And so they did. The woman and her daughter deftly wove a reed basket, thinking how fortunate they were to be able to contribute to the mitzvah of *bikkurim*.

There was a wealthy man who owned several orchards. One day a farmhand told him, "Some of the fruits are turning ripe."

"So what?" the wealthy man asked.

"Well, don't you have to take some fruit to the Temple?"

"Oh, for heaven's sake!" the wealthy man said. "I can't be running to Jerusalem all the time. I have things here to take care of. But I guess it can't be avoided." After a few moments he added, "You know some-

Poor but Worthy / 157

thing? Last year, there was a man who brought his *bikkurim* in a silver vessel. I'm going to bring my *bikkurim* in a gold vessel. Let him *plotz* with envy!"

Rebbe David said, "The reed baskets that were woven with love for Hashem were kept in the Temple. The gold and silver vessels that were brought to show off one's wealth and to elicit the envy of others were returned to their owners. Hashem has no use for these."

That is why the Talmud says that the woven baskets were kept, while the silver and gold ones were returned.

MORE ABOUT SENSITIVITY

I noted above how grave a sin it is to hurt a person's feelings, citing the Midrash that the decree of Haman was enacted because Jacob had caused Esau grief when he took Isaac's blessings intended for Esau. Here is an elaboration of that theme.

The *Yalkut* says that Moses resisted accepting the mission to liberate the Israelites from Egypt (*Exodus* Chs. 3-4) because he was afraid that his older brother, Aaron, would be offended that he was passed over. R' Nosson Zvi Finkel, the Alter of Slobodka, commented, "Hundreds of thousands of Jews were cruelly enslaved and their children were being killed, and Moses is concerned not to hurt his brother's feelings!" Indeed, Hashem assured Moses that Aaron would be happy for him.

An official from a free-loan society in Israel consulted the Chazon Ish. A man had borrowed a large sum of money, and he had given his wife's jewelry as a pledge. The man was unable to repay the loan. Could they sell the jewelry, since the society needed the money to provide loans to other needy people?

The Chazon Ish was stunned. "A free-loan society that puts pledges up for sale would have better never existed!" he said.

"Just imagine," the Chazon Ish said, "that you sold the jewelry, and the woman who had owned it meets another woman wearing her jewelry. Can you imagine her pain and shame? Can there ever be forgiveness for causing a person so much suffering?"

We must be extremely cautious not to hurt anyone's feelings.

THE SEARCH FOR TRUTH

Several times the Talmud refers to a verse in the Torah as being all encompassing. Such verses include, "'You shall love your fellow as yourself' is an all-inclusive rule of Torah" (Jerusalem Talmud *Nedarim* 9:4), and "Which is a small verse in the Torah on which the entire Torah depends? Know Him in all your ways'" (*Berachos* 63a). I believe yet another verse is all encompassing: "All the ways of a person are right in his own eyes" (*Proverbs* 21:2). This verse affects every aspect of a person's behavior.

A person's adjustment to reality is totally dependent on his or her perception of reality. Cognitive psychology has demonstrated that many problems are due to people's misperception of reality. If a person's vision is faulty and he cannot see the open pit before him, there is no doubt that he will be injured.

We are often victims of self-deception. When we have a desire to do something, the defense mechanisms in our subconscious minds can develop ingenious reasons why what we wish to do is right and proper. This is termed *rationalization*. We concoct logical reasons for what we wish to do and we believe them, and if criticized, we vigorously defend our misconceptions.

Rabbi Eliyahu E. Dessler, in *Michtav M'Eliyahu (Search for Truth)*, has a powerful essay on "The Perspective of Truth." He cites the Torah statement, "A bribe will blind the eyes of the wise and make just words crooked" (*Deuteronomy* 16:19). We are all bribed by our desires, and we cannot think objectively. We rationalize our behavior. The Talmud says that even the minutest bribe can bring about a distortion of judgment.

The Torah says that if a judge accepts a bribe, "his eyes are blinded" (*Deuteronomy* 16:19). We are all "bribed" by our desires, and therefore, our perception of reality is distorted. We see many things the way we want them to be rather than how they, in fact, are.

> The *Tzaddik* of Apt was a judge in a litigation that went on for several days. Abruptly, he withdrew from the case, saying he had lost his objectivity.
>
> On Friday evening, when he put on his Sabbath *kaftan*, he found an envelope filled with money. One of the litigants had put it into the *Tzaddik's* pocket. He said, "Now I understand why I lost my objectivity. A litigant had tried to bribe me by putting money in my *kaftan*. Even though I did not discover the bribe until several days later, my thinking had shifted to favoring him. I did not know why this was happening, but I felt that I had lost my objectivity. That is the power of a bribe. It can distort your judgment even if you are unaware of the bribe."

How much more so are we subject to distortion when the "bribe" is within us, and has the power of a strong desire!

Did Bilaam really think he could outsmart Hashem? Bilaam was no fool. He was told in no uncertain terms that Hashem would not allow him to curse Israel, and he obviously knew the infinite power of Hashem. Yet, his hatred for Israel distorted his judgment, and he tried to do what he logically knew he could not do.

If we wish to do what is right, we must be on the alert and on the defensive. Our defense mechanisms operate in the subconscious part of our minds, which is "cunning, baffling, and powerful," as addiction is described. We must exercise our conscious mind to the limit with prayer and *mussar* to avoid self-deception.

A recovering alcoholic said, "In all my years of drinking, I never once took a drink unless I decided it was the right thing to do at the time." The most destructive behaviors can appear to be correct when we have a desire to do them.

This poses an almost insoluble problem. Inasmuch as we are always motivated by a desire for something, how can one ever know that what one is doing is in fact right? The answer is that there is never any certainty. All one can do is minimize the likelihood of error.

> The Rebbe of Rizhin advised a chassid, "The way a tightrope walker keeps his delicate balance is that when he feel a tug to the left, he leans a bit to the right. Similarly, when you have a desire to do something, think of reasons why you should *not* do it."

Another way to avoid an error in judgment is to consult another person, who is not subject to the "bribe" of *your* desires. He may have his own biases, but he is not affected by yours.

King Solomon was so right. "All the ways of a person are right in his own eyes." If we keep this in mind, we may avoid making bad judgments.

DO WE BLESS HASHEM?

Many times each day, we say, *Baruch Atah Hashem*, which can be translated, "Blessed are You, Hashem." But just what does it mean that Hashem is blessed? Some authorities interpret this to mean that "Hashem is the Source of all blessing." Yet others take it literally, that *we bless Hashem*.

The grounds for this rather strange interpretation is the Talmud's statement (*Berachos* 7a) that Rebbe Yishmael *Kohen Gadol* once entered the Holy of Holies, and heard Hashem say, "Yishmael, my child, bless Me." Inasmuch as Hashem is absolute perfection, how can He possibly need a blessing?

The answer may be found in a Midrash (*Eichah Rabbah* 1:35) which states that when the Children of Israel do the will of Hashem, they increase the strength of Hashem. Another enigmatic statement. How can Hashem's strength be increased?

Bnei Yisasschar cites the verse in *Proverbs* (29:4), "By justice does a king establish his land," and states that Hashem conducts the world according to His system of justice, and never steps out of the parameters of justice. When Israel is undeserving, Hashem may maneuver matters so that He can bestow His kindness upon them, but it is always within the confines of justice.

Inasmuch as Hashem is Absolute Goodness, He wants to bestow His kindness upon us. However, when we disobey His will, His system of justice prevents Him from doing so because we have erected obstacles, so that the kindness Hashem radiates cannot reach us. Although we cannot really ascribe emotions to Hashem, the Torah and the Talmud nevertheless refer to Hashem being "angry," "happy," or "sad." In the same vein, we can speak of Hashem as being "frustrated" when we prevent His kindness from reaching us.

When we fulfill Hashem's will, we eliminate the barriers between us and Hashem, and allow His kindness to reach us. We are enabling Hashem to carry out His desire, and in this sense, we are, as it were, "increasing the strength" of Hashem.

When we recite *berachos*, acknowledging the omnipotence and majesty of Hashem, we can think of this as "blessing" Hashem. The words *"Baruch Atah Hashem"* can thus be taken literally.

EMUNAH (FAITH)

Rambam cites belief in the existence of Hashem (*emunah*) as a mitzvah. The question then arises: Did Moses fulfill the mitzvah of *emunah*? One does not have to *believe* that the sun exists, because we can see it; thus we *know* it exists. Belief can only apply to something whose existence is not known to us by a sensory experience. Inasmuch as Moses conversed with Hashem "face to face" (*Exodus* 33:11), he *knew* that Hashem existed. How, then, could he fulfill the mitzvah of *believing* in Hashem?

The answer is that the mitzvah of *emunah* goes beyond believing in the existence of Hashem. It also refers to believing that Hashem's judgment is perfect, even when some things in the world appear to us as grossly unjust. The *Book of Job* poses the vexing question of why the innocent suffer. Several arguments are presented to explain this, but all are rebutted. Ultimately, Hashem says to Job, "Where were you when I created the world?" In other words, understanding why some things happen would require infinite knowledge, which no human can have.

The Talmud states that when Moses said to Hashem, "Let me know Your ways" (*Exodus* 33:13), he was asking for an explanation for why righteous people suffer (*Berachos* 7a), but this wish was not granted. Moses, therefore, had the mitzvah of believing that Hashem's judgment is just and perfect, and he expressed this in his last words to Israel, "Perfect is His work, for all His paths are justice" (*Deuteronomy* 32:4).

This addresses the question, when the Israelites witnessed the Splitting of the Reed Sea, the Torah says, "They believed in Hashem and in His servant, Moses" (*Exodus* 14:31). Seeing the Divine miracle with their own eyes, how could they "believe"? The answer is that the Israelites had suffered decades of torture at the hands of the Egyptians, but when they realized that Hashem is in control of the world, they realized that everything that had happened to them was just, although it was beyond their understanding.

When we suffer adversity, our *emunah* is often challenged. We should remember that the mitzvah of *emunah* applies precisely to that which we cannot know and understand.

FULFILLING ONE'S POTENTIAL

True happiness can be had only when a person fulfills his or her potential. Failure to do so is experienced as a deficiency, subconsciously if not consciously. The problem is that because we are not aware of the enormity of our potential, we do not make the requisite effort to live up to it.

There is a remarkable Midrash on the verse, "You shall be holy," which states, "You might think that you can be as holy as I. No, My holiness is superior to yours" (*Vayikra Rabbah* 24:9), This appears to border on absurdity. How could anyone possibly think the unthinkable, that a mortal's holiness could equal that of Hashem?

Rav Chaim Shmulevitz cites the Talmud that the mother of the prophet Samuel prayed for "an average child, not too bright and not too dull." When she said to Eli, "This is the child I prayed for," she meant "I received what I asked for." The prophet Samuel, who was equivalent to Moses and Aaron combined, was a person of just average ability! (*Sichos Mussar* 5731:18).

Everyone is engaged in the pursuit of happiness. Some people seek happiness in wealth, others in acclaim. Some people in desperation to experience happiness resort to stimulating the brain with chemicals, or seeking the thrills of destructive behavior, such as gambling. Most people accept themselves as they are, and do not strive for spirituality.

When Hashem created man, "He breathed a breath of life into him" (*Genesis* 2:7). *Zohar* explains that when one exhales, one exhales from within himself; hence, the term "He breathed a breath of life into him" means that Hashem imparted something of Himself into man. Each of us has capabilities that are virtually infinite, but we fail to cultivate them

We would be more successful in our quest for happiness if we sought self-fulfillment, but this requires a true awareness of the self.

TEFILLAH (PRAYER) BETWEEN MAN AND HASHEM?

The mitzvos are generally classified as those *bein adam laMakom* (between man and G-d) and *bein adam lechaveiro* (between man and his fellow man). We generally think of *tefillah* as being a pure relationship between man and G-d. However, the Ari z"l said that prior to praying, one should say, "I take upon myself the fulfillment of *Veahavta l'rei'acha kamocha* (You shall love your fellow as yourself." Rabbi Akiva said that this mitzvah encompasses all of Torah (Jerusalem Talmud *Nedarim* 9:4). Indeed, in many *siddurim* (prayer books), the morning service is prefaced by Psalm 15:

> *A psalm by David. Hashem. Who may sojourn in Your tent? Who may dwell on Your Holy Mountain? One who walks in perfect*

innocence, and does what is right, and speaks the truth from his heart; who has no slander on his tongue, who has done his fellow no evil, nor cast disgrace upon his close one; in whose eyes a contemptible person is repulsive, but who honors those who revere Hashem; who can swear to his detriment without retracting, who lends not his money on interest; nor takes a bribe against the innocent. The doer of these shall not falter forever.

The Talmud states that King David condensed the 613 mitzvos of the Torah into the provisions of this psalm (*Makkos* 24a).

The Baal Shem Tov was asked, "How can one come to love Hashem, since one can not see Him or have any sensory experience of Him?" The Baal Shem Tov answered, "Love your fellow man, and love of Hashem will follow."

R' Elimelech of Lizhensk composed a beautiful introductory "Prayer Before Prayer," in which he pleads for closeness to Hashem, and says, "Guard us against envying one another, so that we should not envy anyone else and others should not envy us. To the contrary, put in our hearts that we should each see the virtues of our fellow people and not their faults, that we should each speak to our fellow in a way that is proper and desirable to You, and that no one should carry any enmity toward his fellow."

Effective communication with Hashem in *tefillah* is contingent on love and respect for other people.

THE PRIMACY OF SIMCHAH

Perhaps the greatest single contribution of the Baal Shem Tov and chassidus to Judaism was the emphasis on the importance of *simchah* and teaching how one can achieve *simchah* under all circumstances.

The Baal Shem Tov lived in a period of Jewish history when many Jews were in a state of despair. This was shortly after the Chmielnicki pogrom, the worst massacre prior to the Holocaust. They were oppressed by a virulently anti-Semitic regime, were not permitted to live in major cities, were deprived of the means to earn a livelihood, and were subject to the brutal whims of the local noblemen. To make matters worse, they suffered from the bitter disillusion of the false Messiah, Shabbatai Zvi, who had raised false hopes of immediate redemption.

Torah education was limited to a select few, and the uneducated Jew felt himself spiritually worthless as well as economically impoverished. It was upon this scene that the Baal Shem Tov appeared, and taught Jews that as bearers of Divine *neshamos,* they were privileged to be children of Hashem and preciously dear to Him. He taught them that with each mitzvah they perform they are fulfilling the Divine purpose of Creation. As we have noted earlier, the Baal Shem Tov said, "When a Jew returns home from a day's hard work and notices, 'It is just moments to sunset. I must *daven* Minchah quickly,' why, angels tremble before the holiness of his prayer."

It is important that *tefillah* should be recited with joy. The *Sefer HaChinuch* and Ramchal in *Mesillas Yesharim* both state that our actions can generate emotion. If one will act in a manner of joy, he will feel joy.

In the morning *tefillah*, we say, "We are fortunate — how good is our portion, how pleasant our lot and how beautiful our heritage!" Let us impart joy to these words. If we say we are fortunate, let us express our happiness. Let us sing these words with a lively melody, and perhaps dance as we do so. Our *tefillah* can take on an entirely different character!

TRUE L'SHEM SHAMAYIM (SINCERE DEVOTION TO HASHEM)

The Talmud says, "All your actions should be *l'Shem Shamayim* — for the sake of Heaven" (*Ethics of the Fathers* 2:17). The Rebbe of Kotzk commented, "*All* your actions means that even the *l'Shem Shamayim* should be *l'Shem Shamayim*."

This is a very piercing comment. There are times a person believes he is acting *l'Shem Shamayim* when, in fact, his intentions are self-centered. The Talmud relates an incident in which two *Kohanim* (priests) were in competition for the privilege of bringing the offering to the Altar, and one pushed the other from the Altar ramp, causing him to suffer a broken leg. The *Kohanim* then instituted a selection process whereby these services were assigned.

A true *l'Shem Shamayim* would not result in injuring another person in order to conduct a service to Hashem.

This is also evident in the rebellion of Korah against Moses and Aaron, when Korah sought the High Priesthood for himself. True *l'Shem Shamayim* would mean that one is only interested that the service be performed, not *who* performs the service.

R' Yisrael of Salant cites the Talmud that "a dispute that is *l'Shem Shamayim* will endure (*Ethics of the Fathers* 5:20)" and comments that this may refer to a spurious *l'Shem Shamayim*, where each party is in fact motivated by self-interest, but presents his argument as though it were *l'Shem Shamayim*. If one were honest enough to admit his true motivation, he might be persuaded to yield his position, but if he contends that he is selfless and his intentions are *l'Shem Shamayim*, he may not concede. After all, one may not yield on an issue that is *l'Shem Shamayim*. That is why such a dispute will endure.

We must be careful when we insist that our actions are truly *l'Shem Shamayim*. We may be deceiving ourselves.

SIMPLE LESSONS, BUT VERY PROFOUND

During its early days, the Chassidic movement encountered opposition from the great Torah authorities. This was but two decades after the disastrous debacle of the false Messiah, Shabbatai Zvi. There was great concern that the charismatic Chassidic leaders, particularly since they expounded on kabbalah, would perchance lead their adherents away from true Torah observance.

R' Shlomo Eiger, a noted Talmudist and a son of the great R' Akiva Eiger, was among those who did not look kindly at the Chassidim. When his son, R' Leibele Eiger, joined the Chassidim of Kotzk, R' Shlomo was disappointed.

> When R' Leibele returned home after an extended period in Kotzk, his father asked, "What did you learn in Kotzk?"
>
> R' Leibele replied, "I learned three things. 1. A human being is a human being, and an angel is an angel. 2. A human being can become even greater than an angel. 3. The Torah begins with *bereishis bara Elokim*, which means that Hashem created the world, but left it to man to develop it."

It is essential that a person should be aware not only of his enormous potential, but also of his limitations and weaknesses. In contrast to angels, who are spiritually perfect, a human being has a *yetzer hara* that tempts him to disobey Hashem's will.

> My great-grandfather, R' Shlomo of Bobov, visited Baron Rothschild in Frankfurt. Rothschild proudly showed the Rebbe that he had a house in which he dwelt only on Passover. No *chametz* ever entered the house.
>
> The Rebbe told him he was missing the point. The Torah did not say to never have *chametz*. Rather, one should have *chametz* and dispose of it before Passover.

The *sefarim* say that *chametz* symbolizes the *yetzer hara* (see following essay). To be without a *yetzer hara* is to be an angel, but that is not what Hashem desired when He created man. One has a *yetzer hara*, but one must become its master.

Some people deny their animalistic drives, disowning feelings that they consider to be beneath their dignity. This is self-deception.

Angels are static, unable to advance beyond the level of spirituality inherent in their creation. Human beings are capable of self-improvement, elevating themselves spiritually.

The psalmist says, "The heavens, the heavens are to Hashem, but the earth He has given to mankind" (*Psalms* 115:16). Hashem made the heavens heavenly, and assigned to humans the task of making the earth heavenly.

Three simple statements, but very far reaching.

MATZAH AND CHAMETZ

A number of foods are *tereifah* (forbidden). According to halachah, if a piece of *tereifah* food falls into a pot of kosher food, and the proportion of kosher to *tereifah* is greater than 60:1, the food may be eaten. This is referred to as *bittul*; i.e., the small amount of *tereifah* food is nullified by the greater amount of kosher food.

On Passover, *chametz* is forbidden, but the principle of *bittul* does not apply. If the tiniest crumb of *chametz* falls into a vat of 10 million gallons of kosher food, the entire 10 million gallons are forbidden. A logical question is: Why is the prohibition of *chametz* on Passover so much harsher than that of all other forbidden foods?

The *Bnei Yisasschar* offers the following explanation. In the baking of matzah, from the moment that the flour and water come in contact, something is always being done to it. The matzah dough is kneaded, rolled flat, perforated, and put into the oven. It is not left untouched for a moment. In fact, if it is left untouched, it is suspected to have become *chametz*.

The baking of bread is different. One mixes the ingredients, then sets it aside for several hours and *allows it to rise*. You cannot do anything to make it rise. It is spontaneous, and it rises without any human input.

Matzah is symbolic of Hashem's absolute control over everything in the world. Hashem has given people the freedom to make moral and ethical choices, and He does not control these actions. Except for this, everything in the world is under the immediate and constant control of Hashem.

Chametz, in contrast, symbolizes spontaneous activity. Something is happening by itself, without anyone doing anything to make it happen. We are permitted to eat *chametz* all year round, but when we celebrate Hashem's delivering us from the bondage of Egypt, *chametz* is forbidden in even the most minuscule proportion. This is meant to teach us that there are no events, not even the slightest happening in the world (except for matters of moral free choice), that happen without the participation of Hashem.

This is why in contradistinction from *tereifah*, *chametz* on Passover is forbidden in even the tiniest amount.

THE DAWN OF LIFE

"Satisfy us in the morning with Your kindness, then we shall sing out and rejoice throughout our days" (*Psalms* 90:14).

My mother asked, "What does morning have to with 'throughout our days?'" She answered, "Morning refers to the dawn of our lives. If we have a happy childhood, we can be happy throughout our lives."

We ask Hashem to satisfy us with kindness in our childhood. The greatest kindness a child can have is the security of a loving home. We must do our part to provide our children with this vital kindness that will set the tone for their entire lives. If we do our part, we can be sure that Hashem will help us succeed.

There is no greater obligation and responsibility in the world than establishing true *shalom bayis*. A husband and wife are two unique individuals, each with his and her own wants and needs, and each convinced that his or her philosophy of life is correct and the way he or she does things (and the way his or her parents did things) is the way things should be done.

In order for there to be a true *shalom bayis*, one that will enable a child to grow up happy, parents must realize that they may have to sacrifice some of their own wants and needs. There must be not only selfless love, but also mutual respect for each other.

Bringing a child into our chaotic, stress-ridden world is an awesome responsibility. The focus in the home ceases to be, "What would I like?" and must become, "What is the healthiest for the child?" If parents do not agree on this, they should seek competent help to eliminate conflicts.

The essential kindness to the child is not manifested in toys, gifts, or candy. It is in the security of knowing he/she has a home that is firm as the Rock of Gibraltar, a home that can withstand the stresses of modern life and one in which the parents' prime motivation is the welfare of the children.

GUT SHABBOS

My dear friends, I know that I am not qualified to deliver *tochachah* (rebuke), yet I must share with you a very troubling observation.

When I walk down the street on Shabbos, and *Baruch Hashem*, there are many people going to shul or coming home from shul, I say "Gut Shabbos" to them. Some respond, "Gut Shabbos," but others look at me as if I had recently landed from Mars. I regularly notice people passing each other, but very few offer a "Gut Shabbos" greeting.

The Talmud relates that the great R' Yochanan ben Zakkai always initiated greeting others, even non-Jews in the marketplace. You can be certain that R' Yochanan ben Zakkai's mind was constantly occupied with Torah, yet he felt it important to greet everyone he met, even non-Jews! Why do we have a problem in that we fail to extend a "Gut Shabbos" to others?

One Erev Yom Kippur, R' Yisrael Salant passed a man on his way to shul, whose facial expression indicated that he was preoccupied with the solemnity of Yom Kippur. R' Yisrael said, "Granted that you are very solemn because you are thinking of *teshuvah*, but is that any reason to deprive me of a pleasant greeting?"

When R' Yosef Chaim Sonnenfeld was a student in the Pressburg yeshivah, his friends noticed that on Friday night, on the way home from shul, he would leave the group and rejoin them a bit later. Curious, two of his friends followed him as he went to the poorer section of town, knocked on the door of a basement apartment where a widow lived, and declared an enthusiastic "Gut Shabbos."

"Who is she to you?" they asked. "Your grandmother or aunt?"

"No," R" Yosef Chaim said, "Just a lonely widow. I try to lift her spirits with a fervent 'Gut Shabbos.'"

As is stated in Scripture, "As water reflects a face back to a face, so one's heart is reflected back to him by another" (*Proverbs* 27:19). All of our actions inspire a like response, and a warm and friendly "Gut Shabbos" will inevitably engender good feelings and camaraderie.

There are many ways of doing *chesed*. Some are costly; some require an expenditure of effort. But it is so simple to smile and say "Gut Shabbos" when you meet someone on Shabbos.

THE VIEW FROM ABOVE

The Talmud (*Pesachim* 50a) relates that R' Yosef was sick and fell into a coma. When he recovered, his father, R' Yehoshua ben Levi, asked him what he had experienced, and he said that he had had a vision of the Next World. "It was inverted," he said. "People who are important here on earth are insignificant there. People who are insignificant here on earth are important there."

His father said, "You have seen a clear world." In other words, it is our world, the earthly world, that is inverted.

Our perception of things is distorted. The Talmud says that in the Next World, the *tzaddikim* will see the *yetzer hara* as being gigantic and will wonder, "How did we ever overcome that?" The *reshaim* (wicked ones) will see the *yetzer hara* as minuscule, and will say, "How foolish that we succumbed to it" (*Succah* 52a).

As R' Yehoshua ben Levi said, the view from above is the correct one.

The Talmud says that the greater a person is, his *yetzer hara* is proportionally greater (ibid.). A spiritual person who is devoted to Hashem and knows that he has a Divine soul is much like a person who is wearing a fine silk garment, and takes great caution that it should not become stained. If he walks through a place where there is much dirt, he is careful that his garment should not become soiled, and he does not see this as an extraordinary effort. A person who is physically indulgent has a tiny *yetzer hara*, yet is unable to resist it. When he sees how easy it would have been to resist the *yetzer hara*, he weeps with remorse, but alas, it is too late.

We may feel that the *yetzer hara* is so powerful that we cannot resist its temptation. This is an illusion.

ATTITUDE AND BEHAVIOR

There are various schools of psychology.

The psychodynamic schools believe that our behavior results from our ideas and emotions. Dysfunctional behavior is due to the ideas and emotions resulting from early life experiences. If a person can be helped to understand the sources of his ideas and emotions, he can see why he is acting in a certain way and change it.

The cognitive behavioral schools focus on changing dysfunctional behavior, and do not emphasize analyzing the sources of the behavior.

The *Sefer HaChinuch* (Mitzvah 16) says that a person's attitude is determined by one's actions. In other words, if you wish to *feel* happy, *act* happy.

As noted earlier, Ramban, in his famous letter to his son, begins by telling him to control his anger. What Ramban is referring to is not the *feeling* of anger, because a person does not have control over his feelings. Rather, Ramban is referring to *rage*, or how one reacts to anger, which is something one is able to control.

Ramban then goes on to say that control of rage will lead to the development of *anivus* (humility), *which is the finest of all character traits.* The obvious question is, inasmuch as *anivus* is the finest of all character traits, why does Ramban suggest a circuitous route to *anivus* via control of rage? Why did he not instruct his son directly to develop *anivus*?

The answer is that *anivus* is an attitude, a feeling, and it is difficult to develop feelings. Controlling rage, however, is an action, which is much easier to do.

The psychological approaches are not an either-or choice. One may begin by making the salutary behavior changes, and then go on to investigate the sources of dysfunctional behavior.

PSYCHOLOGY AND JUDAISM

I am often consulted by psychology students or by young people who are considering a career in psychology regarding the compatibility of psychology with Torah. There is legitimate reason for their concern. The quantum leap in modern psychology occurred in the early 20th century, when the theories of Sigmund Freud were widely accepted.

Freud was a brilliant thinker, and made invaluable contributions to our understanding of the way the human mind functions. He elucidated the workings of the unconscious mind and the way its defense mechanisms operate. However, Freud was not only an atheist, but was anti-religion, considering religion to be a neurosis. Obviously, the duty of a psychotherapist is to cure a person's neuroses. Therefore, to his way of thinking, a therapist must help a client dispense with his religion. It is obvious that this psychological orientation is unacceptable to a religious person.

In the latter half of the 20th century, psychology underwent a significant change. While some of Freud's theories have been retained, Freudian psychology no longer prevails. Cognitive psychology and behaviorism have become the popular modalities, and these are not anti-religion. We now have hundreds of competent psychotherapists who are Torah observant. Nevertheless, a Torah-observant psychotherapist and anyone seeking psychological counseling must develop a relationship with a Rav with whom he or she may consult should issues involving religion arise.

A therapist should not lose sight of the fact that there is more to psychological health than freedom from distressing symptoms. In *Happiness and the Human Spirit,* I called attention to the Spirituality Deficiency Syndrome, and it is important that therapists should be aware of this.

A human being is a composite creature, comprised of a body and a spirit. The body, for all intents and purposes, is essentially an animal body. The physical body requires essential nutrients, whose lack will result in symptoms. Thus, lack of iron, vitamin C, and vitamin D will produce conditions recognized as iron deficiency syndrome, vitamin C deficiency syndrome, and vitamin D deficiency syndrome, respectively. The physician is alert to these conditions, can test for them, diagnose them, and prescribe the missing nutrient. Failure to prescribe the specific missing nutrient will result in lack of recovery.

The human spirit is the component that gives a person his uniqueness as a human being. I.e., the spirit is comprised of traits that are lacking in animals, such as:

- the ability to think of a goal and purpose in life
- the ability to improve oneself
- the ability to sacrifice one's comfort or possessions for the welfare of others
- the ability to forgive
- the ability to make moral and ethical judgments
- the ability to deny bodily drives that are in conflict with morals and ethics

- the ability to search for truth
- the ability to admit to having made a mistake
- the ability to control one's anger

These and several other traits are not found in animals, and they comprise the human *spirit*, which is an integral component of a human being.

Just as the body requires its nutrients and develops symptoms of a deficiency syndrome when any essential nutrient is lacking, so the spirit requires its nutrients, and a lack of these will result in a "spirituality deficiency syndrome" (SDS).

A person who is deficient in spirituality is incomplete as a human being. The symptom of SDS is *chronic discontent and unhappiness*. These are not treatable with antidepressant medications, and are relieved only when a person provides his spirit with its nutrients, which consist of *implementing the traits that comprise the human spirit*.

Religion is indeed essential to a wholesome life, but it is separate from spirituality. In courses in psychology we are taught that a therapist should not address religion. I agree. Religion should be addressed by religious authorities. However, spirituality should definitely be addressed by a therapist, just as nutrition is addressed by a physician.

People experiencing the discontent of SDS may turn to any of a variety of things that will relieve this misery. Some may turn to alcohol or drugs, others to food, others to gambling, others to pursuit of wealth, others to pursuit of glory, others to control and domination of others. Any of these may provide temporary relief. Indeed, a person who suffers from symptoms of vitamin deficiency may obtain temporary relief from alcohol or tranquilizers, but as soon as this relief wears off, the misery returns. Similarly, any of the defenses against the discontent of SDS provide only temporary relief, with return of the discontent.

It is natural for a person experiencing discontent to look for what has caused it. He is prone to blame anything that comes to mind and seek to eliminate the cause while ignoring his own role in the discontent. He may blame his job and seek work elsewhere. He may blame his community and try a geographic cure. He may blame his spouse, file for divorce, and seek relief in a new relationship.

As therapists, we are taught to seek the causes of a person's emotional symptoms, but nowhere are we taught to investigate whether a person may be suffering from SDS. We do not hesitate to ask questions about a person's most private and intimate behaviors, but not too frequently does a therapist ask, "What do you see as an ultimate purpose in your life?" or "How careful are you in making sound moral and ethical judgments and living by them?" or any of the other spiritual traits. A therapist may have the attitude is that it is not his place to give his clients *mussar*. Maybe not. But it *is* the therapist's place to investigate whether a person is violating his own moral standards.

In seeking the sources of a person's emotional symptoms, and failing to consider SDS, a therapist may place the blame on faulty parenting. The latter may indeed be a contributing factor in the client's problems, but in failure to recognize SDS, a therapist may exaggerate the parent-child relationship, resulting in the client seeing his parents as villains, and severing the relationship of the client to his parents.

It is the Torah emphasis on the definition of a person as comprised of *guf* and *neshamah*, body and soul, that provides the foundation for wholesome therapy. Interestingly, when we pray for a person's recovery, we pray for *refuas hanefesh urefuas haguf* (healing of the spirit and healing of the body), giving primacy to the spirit. It will well serve a Torah-observant therapist to keep this in mind, because, unfortunately, it is overlooked in the customary psychological training.

ADAPTING TO ADVERSITY

We pray that Hashem does not test us. In our morning prayers we say, "He Who bestows beneficent kindnesses on His people Israel." Isn't "beneficent kindness" redundant? Every kindness is beneficent, isn't it? Not quite. There are blessings in disguise. Great *tzaddikim,* such as Nachum Ish Gamzu, could accept the greatest adversities as kindnesses. We may not be able to aspire to that, so we pray for beneficent kindnesses, the type that comes in an attractive wrapper and tastes sweet.

But we may nevertheless encounter difficult situations in life. We might reflect on the verse in *Micah* (7:8), "Do not rejoice over me, my enemy, for though I fell, I will rise. Although I sit in the darkness, Hashem is a light unto me." The Midrash (*Shochar Tov Tehillim* 5) comments, "Had I not fallen, I would not have risen. Had I not been in the dark, Hashem would not be my light."

We cannot fathom the ways of Hashem. The *sefarim* tell us that when a person is standing upright, he may not be able to see a precious jewel on the ground. When Hashem causes us to fall, it may be so that we can discover something valuable.

> At a meeting of recovering alcoholics, one person said, "I am wise to the pattern. Every adversity I experienced has been followed by something good. Now, when something bad happens, I get excited awaiting the good that is going to come."
>
> I envied this person's faith.

The greatest danger is to fall into a depression. While we may not have the spirituality of Nachum Ish Gamzu and welcome all adversities as blessings in disguise, we should strengthen our *emunah* and believe that something good will come of them.

STANDARDS OF LIVING

Rambam says that a person is influenced by his environment. We are particularly subject to such an influence in regard to our standards of living. There is no question that most of us could survive on much less, but we place stress upon ourselves to acquire things that are not essentials of life.

In the morning *tefillah,* we say, "Happy is one whose help is the G-d of Jacob, whose hope is to Hashem" (*Psalms* 146:5). Why did King David invoke the patriarch Jacob instead of Abraham? Because it was Jacob who prayed for Hashem to provide him with "bread to eat and clothes to wear" (*Genesis* 28:20). Jacob did not pray for delicacies or designer clothing, just for the bare necessities of life.

Yes, one who seeks nothing more than what Jacob sought can indeed be a happy person. We may deceive ourselves by saying that *we* could get along with much less, but that we must provide adequately for our children. R' Bunim of Pshische said that when the child who was the recipient of the father's frenetic lifestyle grows up, he, too, claims he could get along with less, but must provide for *his* children. "Where," R' Bunim asked, "is that ultimate child, for whom so many generations have expended their energies?'

R' Shneur Zalman of Liadi said, "What the Torah forbids is indeed prohibited, but much of what is permissible is unnecessary."

What I have learned from my work with addicts is that they are never satisfied, always looking for more and more to satisfy their cravings. This is not unique to addicts. If we will be honest with ourselves, we will realize that we, too, may have bottomless pits, never satisfied with what we have.

We would do well to listen to our prayers. "Happy is one whose help is the G-d of Jacob"; Jacob, who asked only for "bread to eat and clothes to wear."

OUR PLEA FOR LIFE

Yes, we do *daven* regularly, but we may not be aware of the power of *tefillah* and its importance.

R' Akiva Eiger wrote in a letter, "I did pray for the person, but my prayer was not answered. Perhaps you did not give me the right name." R' Akiva Eiger was sure that his prayer would have been effective had he had the person's correct name.

You may say, "Yes, that was R' Akiva Eiger, but that does not apply to my prayer." Doesn't it? We say in the *Amidah* "for You listen to the prayer of every mouth of Your people Israel with compassion." All our prayers are heard.

We may not give our prayer the *kavannah* it is due. In his introductory prayer, R' Elimelech of Lizhensk states that the *yetzer hara* distracts us from concentrating "even when we are praying for our very lives." Yes, our thoughts often wander during *tefillah,* but can you imagine a person pleading before a judge to spare his life, yet thinking about anything else?

We say in our morning prayer, "To You, Hashem, I would call, and to the L-rd I would appeal. What gain is there in my death, in my descent to the pit? Will the dust acknowledge You? Will it declare Your truth?" (*Psalms* 30:9-10). Listen to the words! We are appealing for our lives by virtue of the fact that we can praise Hashem only when we are alive. In other words, if we fail to praise Hashem, we forfeit the right to life. How can we allow the *yetzer hara* to distract us when our very lives are hanging in the balance?

If we give proper attention to the words we say in *tefillah*, our prayers can be very powerful.

A UNIQUE INTERPRETATION

The reason I am sharing this with you is because I believe that anything we know about our *gedolim*, even anecdotes, should be recorded for posterity. Inasmuch as this incident occurred in 1952, the number of people who remember it is dwindling.

I was at an Agudath Yisrael convention at the Pioneer Hotel in Greenfield Park, NY. When I remember that I was in a room together with the *gedolim* — Rav Aharon Kotler, Rav Moshe Feinstein, Rav Yitzchak Yaakov Ruderman, Rav Yaakov Kamenetzky, Rav Mendel Kaplan, Rav Eliezer Silver, and the Novominsker Rebbe — my head spins.

You can imagine what kind of a Shabbos it was, with *divrei Torah* by these Torah giants. Shabbos night, there was a plenary session which hundreds of people attended.

The speaker at this session was Rav Pinchas Teitz. At one point,

Rav Teitz said that "Agudah must go in a new direction," at which point Rav Aharon Kotler jumped up, took the microphone from Rav Teitz and began shouting, "Never! Agudah will never change its ways. Agudah was founded by the *gedolei hador* and will always remain the same." He continued, and although we were not able to make out all of his words, it was obvious what he was saying. With that, the session broke up.

We came together again at 12:30 a.m. for the *melavah malkah*, at which Rav Eliezer Silver spoke. Rav Silver said,

"I know you are all upset about the interchange between Rav Teitz and the Kletzker Rosh Yeshivah. I am here to tell you that Rav Teitz was right.

"The Torah says that the *parah adumah* [the red heifer used in the ritual to purify someone who had come in contact with the dead] must be totally red. Even two black hairs disqualify it.

"Whoever heard of such a thing? Throughout halachah, the rule is that we go according to the majority and disregard the minority. According to this, a heifer that is mostly red should be kosher. Even Reb Meir, who says that we must consider a minority, concedes that a minuscule minority is of no concern. That just two black hairs should disqualify a red heifer has no counterpart anywhere in Torah.

"There are varying degrees of *tumah* [ritual contamination]. There is the *av*, a primary source of *tumah*, and several *toldos* (secondary levels) in which the *tumah* is attenuated. In general, the rule of the majority composition prevails. However, there is the *tumah* of the dead body, which is the *avi avos hatumah*, the highest degree and intensity of *tumah*, which is so severe that the usual rules do not apply. The means to counteract this intense *tumah* can be disqualified by something so minuscule as two black hairs.

"Agudah never advocated *kannaus* [zealousness]. Agudah always stood firm and unyielding on halachah, but was always tolerant and did not advocate aggressive zealousness. But this was in days when the *tumah* that prevailed in the environment was moderate. Today, with the unprecedented *tumah* that surrounds us in the culture in which we live, Agudah must become aggressively zealous, striking out with great force wherever there is a breach of traditional Torah values.

"This is the new direction of which Rav Teitz spoke."

Rav Aharon Kotler arose and embraced Rav Teitz, to a standing ovation.

COMMITMENT

True achievement requires commitment. And what is commitment? It is a determination to get things done, with no loopholes or bail-out provisions.

Commitment is the antithesis of procrastination. Ramchal says of procrastination, *"ein sakanah kesakanto"* (there is no danger as great as that of procrastination (*Mesillas Yesharim, Zerizus*). If a person decides that he just does not want to do something, he is being honest with himself. If he procrastinates, he is saying, "I will do it, but not just now," and that is self-deception.

We should realize what our weaknesses are and take the necessary steps to overcome them.

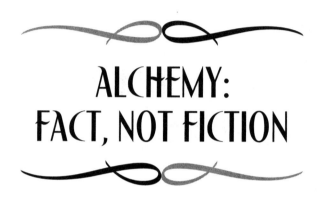

ALCHEMY: FACT, NOT FICTION

For centuries, alchemists tried to convert lead into gold. They searched for the "philosopher's stone," which was said to enable such a transformation. Fairy tales related spinning straw into gold. People fantasized that one could transform worthless items into things of value.

But, of course, that is all fiction. Or is it? The Talmud says that if a person does *teshuvah* out of an intense love for Hashem, his sins, even intentional sins, are transformed into merits (*Yoma* 86b)!

> R' Levi Yitzchak of Berditchev once met a profligate sinner and said to him, "How I envy you! You will have such great reward in Heaven."
>
> The man said, "Rabbi, why do you mock me? You know that I do not observe Torah at all."

"Yes," R' Levi Yitzhak said, "I know. But the Talmud says that when one does *teshuvah* out of an intense love for Hashem, his sins, even intentional sins, are transformed into merits. One day, you will come to your senses and do sincere *teshuvah*. All your sins will then be converted to merits. I could never have as many merits from mitzvos as you will have from your transformed sins!"

The question is: How does one achieve such a level of *teshuvah*? The Baal Shem Tov said that if a person develops true *ahavas Yisrael*, this will lead to *ahavas Hashem*. All we must do is set aside our self-centeredness and develop true love for others, helping the needy and empathizing with those who suffer. We can then acquire a wealth of merits!

HOW IS THIS ALCHEMY ACCOMPLISHED?

Inasmuch as the Talmud says that *teshuvah* that is motivated by an intense love for Hashem can transform intentional sins into merits, I must accept that this is so. Yet, I was always bothered: How could eating *tereifah* ever become a merit, even with the finest *teshuvah*? Let me share with you what may be a solution to this question.

The Chida (*Devash Lefi* 5) relates that the Ohr HaChaim once saw a powerful, wealthy man insult a *talmid chacham*. He suggested to the *talmid chacham* that he forgive this man's rudeness. The *talmid chacham* said, "I promptly forgave him. The *Zohar* says that Jews' sins weigh heavily on the *Shechinah* [Divine Presence]. I realized that every moment this sin exists, it causes distress to the *Shechinah*, and I did not want the

Shechinah to be distressed because of me." The Ohr HaChaim profusely praised this *talmid chacham*.

The Torah says that it is a mitzvah to relieve an animal of its burden (*Exodus* 23:5). *Sefer HaChinuch* says this mitzvah is to teach us compassion, and we certainly should have compassion for people who are burdened, R' Yeruchem Levovitz places extraordinary emphasis on *nosei be'ol im chaveiro* (sharing the burden of one's fellow), and says that this is fundamental to all mitzvos, both to those between man and his fellow man and those between man and Hashem (*Daas Chochmah U'Mussar* Vol.4, p. 29).

If it is a mitzvah to relieve an animal of its burden, and an even greater mitzvah to relieve a human being of his burden, just think how great a mitzvah it is, as the *talmid chacham* said, to relieve Hashem of His burden (so to speak)!

Therefore, when an individual does *teshuvah* out of compassion for Hashem, achieving forgiveness for his sins, he has an extraordinarily great mitzvah of relieving Hashem of His burden. Hence, with each sin for which he gains forgiveness, he has a mitzvah! In this way, he achieves a merit for each sin that is forgiven.

A CULTURAL INSANITY

What is insanity? *A minority of one.* If one person has an idea with which no one else agrees, he may be thought to be insane. If many people share the same idea, it is considered normal.

I have worked with addicts for over forty years. The characteristic of addiction is that it is a bottomless pit. There is never a limit to the amount of alcohol or drugs they crave.

King Solomon said, "A lover of money will never be satisfied with money" (*Ecclesiastes* 5:9). This is no different from any other addiction.

A man consulted a psychiatrist. "What is your problem?" the doctor asked.

"I don't have any problems," the man answered.

> "Then why have you come to see me?" the doctor asked.
>
> "Because my family said I should," the man answered.
>
> "What does your family think is the problem?" the psychiatrist asked.
>
> "They think there is something wrong because I like pancakes," the man said.
>
> "That's absurd," the psychiatrist said. "There is nothing wrong with liking pancakes. I like pancakes myself."
>
> The man's eyes lit up. "You really do? Then you should come to my house. I have crates full of pancakes in my attic."

We will readily agree that this person is crazy. If you make a few extra pancakes and put them in the freezer to have ready for breakfast, that is normal. Pancakes have value as something to be eaten. When they are stored in crates in the attic, that is crazy.

Money has value when it can be used to buy things one wants. But if one has so much money that he can never use it all to acquire things, yet amasses more and keeps on adding to it, why is that any different from amassing pancakes in the attic? It is just that society has made the judgment that hoarding pancakes is crazy, but hoarding money is not.

If a person were to spend $3000 every day, he would spend one million dollars in one year. If he has a billion dollars, he would have to live *one thousand years* to spend it all. Yet, which multibillionaire is not engaged in increasing his wealth? Logical thinking will tell you that this is insanity.

> An apocryphal story attributed to both John D. Rockefeller and John Paul Getty has a reporter asking, "Sir, how much money is enough?"
>
> The multimillionaire famously replies, "Just a little more."

We may not have the desired degree of *bitachon* and we may put away some money for a rainy day. That is not insane. But we should not allow society's values to make us into addicts or into pancake stockpilers.

BASIC CHINUCH

I came across a quotation that deeply impressed me. "The most important function of education at any level is to develop the personality of the individual and the significance of his life to himself and to others" (Grayson Kirk, former president of Columbia University).

This is something that cannot be delegated to an educational institution, regardless of how wonderful it may be. It is the job of the home. Furthermore, there are no specific methods or actions that parents should or should not do to achieve this. This is accomplished more by the *attitude* of the parents than by what they do.

Ramchal begins *Mesillas Yesharim* with the chapter, "The Obligation of a Person in One's World," and proceeds to explain what that is. Essentially, it is what Job referred to: A person is born into the world as a "wild mule" (*Job* 11:12) and must become a *mentsch*, which will enable him to become close to Hashem.

When we have a primary goal, all our efforts are directed toward achieving that goal. When I went to medical school, I could not allow anything to distract me from my goal. Everything I did had to be directed toward achieving that goal.

True, we do mitzvos and avoid *aveiros*. That is indeed commendable, but it does not necessarily convey to the children that our entire life, everything we do, is directed toward growing ever closer to Hashem. If children do not develop this feeling, they are vulnerable to any of the pleasure-seeking behaviors so prevalent in our culture.

I am a strong advocate of reading about the lives and behaviors of our great *tzaddikim*, and sharing this with our children. We cannot dismiss this by saying, "I cannot be as great as the Chofetz Chaim." We must strive to perfect ourselves the way the *tzaddikim* did, regardless of how much we actually achieve.

Unfortunately, too many children go "off the *derech* (stray from the right path)." Sometimes it is because we have not really demonstrated to them a Torah-true *derech*.

WASTED OPPORTUNITIES

The Talmud relates that there was a profligate sinner, Elazar ben Durdia. At one point, he had a sudden insight into the depth of moral corruption to which he had sunk, and he began to weep in remorse. His *teshuvah* was so intense that he burst into tears until his soul departed. A voice from heaven declared, "R' Elazar ben Durdia has now been readied for the life of the World to Come." When R' Yehudah HaNasi (the Prince) heard this, he wept, saying, "A person can acquire the World to Come in a single moment" (*Avodah Zarah* 17a).

Why did R' Yehudah weep? Because if one can acquire a portion in the World to Come in a brief period of time, just think how much one could acquire if one would spend much time in *teshuvah* and in doing mitzvos. How tragic it is that people waste so much time.

Suppose that a person who was permitted to help himself to gold nuggets picked up just one nugget and left to entertain himself with the proceeds. We would say, "How foolish that person is, neglecting the opportunity to enrich himself by gathering more gold nuggets, and instead going off to worthless amusement."

Think of how much time we may spend on pastimes or in idle conversations, time that could be used in Torah study and performance of mitzvos. We satisfy ourselves by taking just one or two nuggets, leaving much wealth behind. How foolish!

EVERYTHING POINTS TO HASHEM

The Talmud says, "One who walks on the road while reviewing a Torah lesson, but interrupts his learning and exclaims, 'How beautiful is this tree,' Scripture considers it as if he bears guilt for his soul" (*Ethics of the Fathers* 3:9). The latter expression actually means that one has forfeited one's right to life, which seems to be a very harsh punishment for remarking on the beauty of a tree.

We may understand this better with a statement by R' Elimelech of Lizhensk. The *sefarim* say that the patriarch Abraham served Hashem primarily with the attribute of *chesed* (lovingkindness), Isaac with *gevurah* (strength; might), and Jacob with *tiferes* (beauty).

R' Elimelech explains, "The patriarch Jacob derived praise of Hashem from whatever he saw, ate, or did. For example, if he would eat something very tasty, he would meditate and think, 'This food is something that was created. And Who placed the good taste into this delicacy? Of course, it was the Blessed Creator. If this delicacy has such good taste, this is a certain indication that in the Creator there is every good taste, without bound or limit.' This is what Jacob thought with regard to everything" (*Noam Elimelech, Bo*).

The fault with the person who interrupted his Torah study to comment on the beauty of the tree is precisely that *he interrupted his learning*. His reaction to the beauty of the tree should have been that of Jacob. "If there is such beauty in the tree, this indicates that there is beauty in the One Who created the tree, a beauty that is without bound or limit." This, too, constitutes Torah learning, and would not at all be an interruption.

We should see the hand of Hashem in all beauty, and praise Him for it.

REVIVIFYING THE LIVING

We believe in the miracle of revivification of the dead in the future. For now, the Rebbe of Kotzk said, we should revivify the living.

As stated above, the human being is a composite creature, comprised of a physical body — which for all intents and purposes is an animal body — and "something else," which is that which gives one the uniqueness of being a human being. This "something else" is the human spirit, which is comprised of all the features that are lacking in other living things, among which are greater intelligence, the ability to have a conscious purpose in life, the ability to improve oneself, the ability to make moral choices in defiance of bodily urges, the ability to forgive, and several others. If a person does not exercise these uniquely human traits, he is essentially living an animal life.

The Sages say, "The wicked are considered dead even when they are alive" (*Berachos* 18b). By this they mean that their humanity is dead, although they are physically alive.

Animals follow their every whim, and seek only to satisfy their physical drives. When a person is physically indulgent, it is very difficult for him to relinquish the pursuit of pleasure and live a more spiritual life.

Convincing a person to become more spiritual is a formidable task. This is what the Rebbe of Kotzk meant by revivifying the living.

Only Hashem can revivify the dead. Our responsibility is to revivify the living.

SENSITIVITY TOWARD WIDOWS

The Torah mandates that we must be cautious to avoid offending anyone, but there is a particularly harsh warning not to aggrieve a widow (*Exodus* 22:21).

One evening, the Rebbe of Vizhnitz took a stroll, accompanied by his *gabbai*, and he stopped at the home of a wealthy Jew, the president of a local bank, who was not among his followers. The man was surprised at the Rebbe's unannounced visit, and welcomed him cordially. When the Rebbe sat silently, the man asked the *gabbai* about the reason for the Rebbe's visit. The *gabbai* said he had not the faintest idea.

After a few moments, the Rebbe rose, bid his host goodbye, and headed for the door. The host could not contain his curiosity and asked, "What was the purpose of the Rebbe's visit to my home?"

The Rebbe said, "I came here to perform a mitzvah."

"But what kind of a mitzvah did the Rebbe do here?" the host asked. "I did not see the Rebbe do anything."

The Rebbe said, "The Talmud says that just as it is a mitzvah to instruct someone to do a good deed, it is equally a mitzvah not to instruct him if one knows the other person will not listen. If I am at my home and you are here, then I would have no opportunity to fulfill the mitzvah of not telling you something you would not obey. That is why I came here and said nothing, so that I fulfilled that mitzvah."

The host said, "But what is it that the Rebbe wished to say to me?"

The Rebbe answered, "I cannot tell you, because if I do, I will lose the mitzvah of refraining from telling you something you would not obey."

The host said, "But why is the Rebbe certain that I would not obey?"

The Rebbe said, "Trust me. I know for certain."

The host could not withstand this. "I promise I will obey. What is it?"

The Rebbe said, "You hold the mortgage on the home of a widow who cannot afford the payments, and you sent her a notice of foreclosure. I wanted to ask you to withdraw that notice, but I knew you would not listen."

The host said, "But Rebbe, even though I am president of the bank, it is not my money that is involved. I merely represent all the depositors. I am obligated to foreclose."

The Rebbe said, "See what you have done to me? I knew you would not listen, so I kept silent. Insisting that I tell you has deprived me of a mitzvah."

The host said, "Very well, Rebbe. I will not take away your mitzvah. I will withdraw the foreclosure."

There is an adage, "Where there is Torah, there is wisdom." The Rebbe proved it to be true.

Shortly before Passover, the Steipler Gaon called a yeshivah *bachur* and told him that a few weeks earlier, a *talmid chacham* had died. "I'm sure that he always had *shemurah* matzos for Passover. The widow may not know how to go about getting *shemurah* matzos. Here, take some of my matzos to her.

"But don't tell her that I sent them to her, because according to halachah, a man should not send gifts to a woman. Just tell her that I gave you matzos to give to whomever you wish."

The greatest Torah scholar of our generation thinks how he may mitigate the suffering of a widow!

TRUTHFULNESS

Many people may consider themselves to be honest and truthful. However, whereas they may be most meticulous about *glatt kosher* and may insist on the highest degree of kosher supervision, they may not be quite as precise in regard to truth. It is good to see how cautious our *gedolim* are in regard to truth.

> R' Avraham Yafan told the Rebbe of Satmar that R' Zundel of Salant had received a request from a former student to pray for his wife's recovery from illness. R' Yisrael told his aide to respond that he would indeed pray for her.
>
> When the aide brought the letter to R' Zundel, the latter said he could not sign it. "I said that *I* would pray for her, but you wrote that *we* would pray for her. I did not say that, and that is not the truth."
>
> The Rebbe of Satmar said, "Yes, Ramban says that a person who prays for someone individually should not say 'we' will pray."

R' Avraham Yafan said that he searched for the source in the Ramban and eventually found it. Pharaoh summoned Moses and Aaron and said that *they* should pray to G-d to remove the plague of the frogs, but Moses responded, "*I* will pray for you" (*Exodus* 8:4-5). Moses did not respond, "*We* will pray for you," as Pharaoh had asked, because his pledge was solely with regard to himself. Indeed, verse 8 states, "Moses cried out to Hashem concerning the frogs He had inflicted upon Pharaoh."

(from *Chayim Sheyeish Bahem*, p.137)

Can you imagine being so dedicated to truthfulness that one watches every word, careful not to say "we" instead of "I"?

BROKENHEARTEDNESS VS. DEPRESSION

"Hashem is the Healer of the brokenhearted, and the One Who binds up [soothes] their depression" (*Psalms* 147:3).

Isn't being brokenhearted a great virtue? The psalmist says, "Hashem is close to the brokenhearted" (*Psalms* 34:19). Why, then, would Hashem "heal" the brokenhearted?

Tanya emphasizes the overwhelming importance of *simchah* in the service of Hashem. Nevertheless, it is true that a person must do a thorough soul-searching to uncover his own character defects so that he may improve upon them. Also, inasmuch as there is no human being, even a *tzaddik*, who is free of all sin, we must become aware of our sins so that we may do *teshuvah*. Awareness of one's shortcomings and one's sins causes one to become remorseful. Why would

Hashem seek to relieve us of these constructive feelings?

Tanya points out that not only are brokenheartedness and depression not identical, they are actually polar opposites. Brokenheartedness is the remorse that stimulates a person to take corrective action for self-improvement. It is a positive force. Depression, on the other hand, is a feeling of resignation and despair. The depressed person thinks, *What purpose is there in trying? I am a failure. Nothing I can do will erase my sins and make me better.*

It is necessary for a person to achieve the desirable brokenheartedness, but one must be careful not to allow the feelings resulting from awareness of one's shortcomings and sins to lead into depression. The healing that Hashem does for the brokenhearted person is to protect him from sinking into depression.

Tanya recommends that a person set aside a specific period of time each day for the soul-searching that leads to brokenheartedness as a catalyst for self-improvement. However, when this period is over, one should have joy in the knowledge that Hashem welcomes one's *teshuvah* and efforts at self-improvement, and one should rejoice at having the privilege to serve Hashem.

SHARING HAPPINESS

There is hardly anything more worthy in the Torah than *gemilas chassadim* (acts of lovingkindness). It is superior even to *tzedakah* (charity), because *tzedakah* is done with one's possessions, whereas *gemilas chassadim* is done with one's person.

We fulfill *gemilas chassadim* when we make a condolence call on mourners (*nichum aveilim*). Ir is also *gemilas chassadim* when one participates in a wedding and shares in the joy of the *chasan* and *kallah*.

No one invites you to be *menachem avel*. You hear that someone has sustained a loss, and you make your *nichum aveilim* visit. Yet, if someone you know marries off their child and you have not been invited to the wedding, you often will not go. Why not?

When my son became a bar mitzvah, I said to a friend, "I did not receive your response card."

He replied, "If I had received an invitation, you would have received a response card." I was flabbergasted. I distinctly remember addressing an invitation to him. I then discovered that several other people had not received invitations. Obviously, those invitations had been lost in the mail.

Ever since then, when a friend makes a wedding or a bar mitzvah and I do not receive an invitation, I attend anyway. Inasmuch as I had not sent a response card, I do not stay for the dinner, but I go to the *chuppah* or to the *davening* in shul, wish him *mazal tov,* and dance along with him. His *simchah* is my *simchah,* too, and I should be there to share it with him.

I suggest you do likewise. Share your friends' *simchos*, invitation or no invitation.

FORGIVENESS

Our *sifrei mussar* are replete with the importance of avoiding offending anyone, and with the need for asking *mechilah* if one has done so. But how much must a person extend himself to gain forgiveness? The *Shulchan Aruch* says that a person should take three people with him to appeal for forgiveness, and if the other party still refuses to forgive, one is absolved (*Orach Chaim* 606).

Our great Torah personalities were often not content to avail themselves with the absolutions of halachah, and went far beyond the halachic requirements. The following anecdote is almost not to be believed.

> In the Shaarei Chesed neighborhood in Jerusalem, there was a *tzaddik* whose wife died. Some time afterward, a *shadchan* (marriage broker) suggested a *shidduch* for him with a widow in the neighborhood.

This woman had a reputation of being an impossibly difficult person, irritable, discontented, and an incessant talker. However, the *tzaddik* agreed to marry her. When his family heard of this, they descended upon him, telling him that this was absolute insanity, and that he was letting himself in for a life of misery.

The *tzaddik* explained, "About twelve years ago, this woman came to our home, and she berated my wife nonstop. It disturbed my learning so much that I asked her to please lower her voice. She felt offended by my remark, so I said, 'I did not mean to offend you. Please forgive me,' but she refused to forgive me, even though I appealed to her several times.

"I believe that if I marry her, she will agree to forgive me."

We have heard all kinds of stories about the *mesiras nefesh* (self-sacrifice) that our *tzaddikim* were able to accept. I believe that this tops them all.

THE AHAVAS YISRAEL OF A ZEALOT

There were indeed *gedolim* who were zealots, and had little tolerance for Jews who were not Torah observant. R' Yosef Chaim Sonnenfeld, the Rav of Jerusalem, was known for his zealousness. He was sharply critical of the non-religious Zionists in Israel.

But we must understand that the zeal of the *gedolim* notwithstanding, their love for all Jews, observant and non-observant, surpassed all bounds. They practiced the Baal Shem Tov's statement, "I wish I had the love for the greatest *tzaddik* that Hashem has for the worst *rasha*."

> R' Moshe Blau related that one day he was walking with R' Yosef Chaim when they saw a procession of young boys and girls from several schools heading their way. The children were carrying Israeli flags and

singing Hebrew songs. They took over the entire street, pushing other pedestrians aside.

R' Blau felt that R' Yosef Chaim would be irritated by this, and suggested that they turn back.

"No," R' Yosef Chaim said. "These are Jewish children!"

As the procession neared them, R' Blau saw that R' Yosef Chaim's lips were moving. He leaned closer and heard him saying, "May Hashem increase upon you, upon you and upon your children! You are blessed to Hashem, Maker of heaven and earth" (*Psalms* 115:14), and tears were rolling down his face. He then said, "May they also have the blessing, 'He will bless those who fear Hashem, the small as well as the great'" (ibid. 13).

King Solomon said it: "Love covers all offenses" (*Proverbs* 10:12).

FOCUSING

You've seen it and I've seen it. A person is able to strike a thick brick with the edge of his hand and break it in two. How does that happen? He has been taught how to channel all his energies into his hand. This is also true of a powerful laser beam, where all the wavelengths of light are focused into a single wavelength.

R' Chaim Shmulevitz found a counterpart to this in the Torah. The patriarch Jacob came upon several shepherds who told him that they could not fetch water from the well because of a heavy boulder that covers the well, and it required all the shepherds working together to move it. Jacob removed the boulder singlehandedly. R' Shmulevitz says he accomplished this by focusing all his energies on a single point (*Sichos Mussar* 5731:5).

Our problem is that we are not focused on a single goal. Our thoughts diverge, jumping from one topic to the next in rapid succession. Our great Torah scholars may not all have been innate geniuses, but all were able to focus their minds totally on Torah.

This is particularly important when working toward a goal. Many people have not even formulated a specific goal in life. They drift in many directions and get nowhere.

Ramchal in *Mesillas Yesharim* begins, "What is a person's obligation in his world?" If a person could set his mind on what he sees is the goal and purpose of his life, the concentration of all his energy on this point would enable him to have great success.

People who strive for happiness, wealth, and success have made these the goals of their lives. What they do not recognize is that these are the by-products of goal-setting, but cannot be goals in themselves.

Many people are fully observant of Torah, yet do not make Torah the goal of their lives. If a person is truly dedicated to Torah wisdom, "Length of days is at its right; at its left, wealth and honor" (*Proverbs* 3:18). These are by-products, to the right and to the left, but the goal itself is Torah.

DETERMINATION

We find two episodes in the Torah that involve spies. Moses sent spies to scout Canaan, and the results of this mission were catastrophic. However, Joshua sent spies on a similar mission and the outcome was eminently successful. Why did the two events have such diametrically opposite endings?

The answer is that Moses' spies went with the intention, "Can we conquer the land or not?" This is evident from their words on their return, "We cannot ascend to that people for it is too strong for us" (*Numbers* 13:31). Joshua's spies had no doubt that they were going to conquer the land. Their question was, "What is the best way to do it?"

If you question whether or not you can do something, you are likely to come up with many reasons why you cannot. If you are determined to do something and are looking for the best way to do it, you will succeed.

We have extraordinary abilities to rationalize, to develop very logical reasons for something that we either want or do not want to do. These reasons can be so convincing that we deceive ourselves into believing them. Once we set our minds to do something, we can find ways to get it done.

It has been said, "Winners have goals. Losers have excuses." The excuses may be very convincing, but one loses anyway.

THE LIFE OF THE WORLD

"Thus the heaven and the earth were finished, and all their array. On the seventh day, Hashem completed His work which He had done" (*Genesis* 2:1-2). Rashi addresses the obvious question: Why does the Torah say that Hashem completed His work on the *seventh* day? Everything was completed on the *sixth* day. Rashi says, the world lacked "rest," and with the rest of Shabbos, the world was completed.

There is a problem with this answer. It may seem that "rest" is a passive condition. If one is not active and not working, then there is rest. Thus, when Hashem abstained from work, there was automatically rest.

That this is not so is evident from the *berachah* we recite, "Who forms light and creates darkness." Light indeed needed to be created, but, one might think, darkness did not require creation. When there is no light, there is automatically darkness. The *sefarim* say that everything in the world required to be created. This is somewhat difficult to understand, but the concept is valid. Darkness was a creation; it was not simply the absence of light. If so, then "rest," too, was not merely abstinence from work, but actually a creation, and this completion, as the Torah says, was done on the seventh day. But inasmuch as Hashem observed His Shabbos, how could have He created rest on Shabbos?

The answer lies in the verse in *Exodus* (31:17), "And on the seventh day, He rested *vayinafash,*" which is loosely translated as "and He was refreshed," hardly a term that can apply to Hashem. Sforno explains *vayinafash* as related to the word *nefesh*, saying that Hashem endowed Shabbos with a soul. What would Shabbos have been without a *nefesh*? Why, it would have been a lifeless Shabbos! Therefore, putting a *nefesh* into Shabbos falls into the category of *pikuach nefesh*, which Hashem was permitted, so to speak, to do on Shabbos!.

This may well be what Rashi meant, "the world lacked 'rest,' and with the rest of Shabbos, the world was completed." The world required the "rest" of Shabbos for its existence; hence, it was a matter of *pikuach nefesh* to create rest on the seventh day.

PURIM — THE ETERNAL FESTIVAL

I could hardly believe that there was such a Midrash, but yes, I saw it with my own eyes. "All the festivals will fall away, but the days of Purim will never fall away, because it says, 'The days of Purim will never pass from among the Jews'" (*Midrash Shochar Tov, Mishlei* 9). How is it possible that the festivals of Passover, Succos, and Shavuos will ever fall away? They are Scriptural mitzvos!

That is a problem with which the Torah commentaries wrestle. But what is undeniable is that Purim is of extraordinary importance, perhaps even superior to the Scriptural festivals.

In a series of essays, *Kedushas Levi* goes to great length to explain the superiority of Purim.

The Scriptural festivals all commemorate supernatural miracles.

Passover: the ten plagues and the Splitting of the Reed Sea. Succos: the Clouds of Glory that surrounded the Israelites in the Wilderness. Shavuos: the Revelation at Sinai. All of these events were manifest miracles in which the hand of Hashem was clearly evident. The waters of the Sea do not divide naturally, Clouds of Glory encircling the encampment are not a natural phenomenon, and the awesome Revelation at Sinai was not, by any stretch of the imagination, a natural event. No one had to have *emunah* that Hashem was doing these things.

Purim, however, was not an obvious miracle. The king became drunk and had the queen executed. She was replaced by a beautiful Jewish woman, Esther, who concealed her origins. The prime minister, Haman, was a vitriolic anti-Semite. A Jewish nobleman, Mordechai, refused to bow to him. Consequently, Haman wished to kill all the Jews. Mordechai overheard a palace intrigue to assassinate the king and thereby saved the ruler's life. Haman schemed to have Mordechai executed, but his attempt to obtain permission to hang Mordechai resulted in the king having Haman hanged instead.

Anyone reading the story of Purim would not logically conclude that Hashem was maneuvering matters to save the Jews. Everything could be explained naturally.

What Purim teaches us is the basis of Judaism. Hashem is in control of the world. What we think of as "natural phenomena" are nothing less than miracles, but because they are regular occurrences, we do not attribute them to the immediate handiwork of Hashem. We put a seed into the ground; it disintegrates and produces a tree that bears fruit year after year. Is that not a miracle? A single microscopic cell develops into a human being, with a brain that has a hundred billion nerve cells, which are multiply interconnected in a wondrous way, and capable of producing masterpieces. Is that not a miracle?

The psalmist says, "Blessed is Hashem, Who alone does wondrous things" (*Psalms* 72:18), upon which the Talmud comments that often the beneficiary of a miracle is not even aware of what G-d has done for him (*Niddah* 31a).

In the *Amidah* we thank Hashem "for Your miracles that are with us every day." Our daily lives are but a series of miracles, which we tend to write off as "natural" happenings.

That is the importance of Purim. We must forever be aware that our lives are completely in the hand of Hashem, and that He performs countless miracles for us every day.

THE POWER OF STORIES

One of the contributions that Chassidus has made to Judaism is to stress the importance of stories about the lives of *tzaddikim*. This is not a new concept; it is in the category of what the Talmud says, "This had been forgotten, but was re-established" (*Succah* 44a). In *Genesis* (24:34-48), the Torah cites Eliezer's lengthy narration of his experience, which is a repetition of what the Torah related earlier. Rashi (ibid. 24:42) cites the Talmudic statement, "The talk of the servants of the patriarchs is dearer to Hashem than the halachic exegeses of their descendants. Eliezer's narration is doubled in the Torah, while many major halachos are derived from slight nuances in the text" (*Sanhedrin* 95a).

Halachos are intellectual concepts that may not arouse emotion. The fundamental principles of love of Hashem and reverence for Hashem are emotions that may not be easily derived from the study of halachos. The ways the *tzaddikim* conducted their lives are powerful teachings that can enable us to develop a relationship to Hashem, so that we may implement the halachos with the proper *kavannah*. Eliezer could describe how the patriarch Abraham lived, and thereby proffer a blueprint for living correctly.

> The Rebbe of Rizhin said, "When the Baal Shem Tov was aware of an impending misfortune, he would go a certain place in the woods to meditate. He would light a fire and say a special prayer, by which the misfortune was averted.
>
> "When his disciple, the Maggid of Mezeritch, had occasion to intercede, he would go to the same place and say, 'Master of the universe! I do not know how to light the fire, but I am still able to say the prayer.' This, too, was effective.
>
> "Still later, R' Moshe Leib of Sasov would go into the woods and say, 'I do not know how to light the fire, and I do not know the prayer, but I do know the place,' and this, too, was sufficient.
>
> "When the Rebbe of Rizhin felt it was necessary to elicit Hashem's compassion, he said, 'Master of the universe! I am unable to light the fire, I do not know the prayer, and I do not even know the place in the woods. All I can do is tell the story, and this must be sufficient.'"

Chassidic lore has it that when we speak about a *tzaddik*, we invoke his great merits. This, too, has its origin in the Talmud, which says that in the Temple, the moment of dawn was announced as, "The eastern sky is brightening all the way to Hebron" (*Yoma* 30b). Hebron was mentioned to invoke the merits of the patriarchs who are buried in Hebron.

And so, at their gatherings, chassidim relate stories about *tzaddikim*. In addition to invoking their merits, the stories are teachings of how to live a Torah-oriented life.

DAVID – THE SWEET MINSTREL OF ISRAEL

Other than the *Chumash* (Five Books of Moses), the most widely used book in Scripture is *Psalms*. In addition to the psalms composed by King David, there are psalms attributed to Adam, Malchizedek, Abraham, Moses, Solomon, Asaph, and the Bnei (descendants of) Korah.

The Midrash states that David prayed that the reciting of his psalms would have the same merit as the study of the most complicated portions of the Talmud (*Midrash Shochar Tov* 1). Again, David prayed that people recite the psalms so that "my lips will move even after my death." Reciting the psalms essentially eternalizes King David. It is noteworthy that of all the great Biblical personalities, it is only of David whom we say, "David, king of Israel, lives and exists."

The Talmud states that David established the "world of *teshuvah*" (*Avodah Zarah* 5a). Indeed, when one reads Psalm 51, one can grasp the elements of *teshuvah*: full confession, profound remorse, and the belief that Hashem accepts *teshuvah* and that in spite of one's misdeeds, he can be in the good graces of Hashem, with restoration of the Divine spirit and a return to joy.

Psalms has been variously divided according to the days of the week and the days of the month. Many chassidim recite the entire *Book of Psalms* every Shabbos.

The psalms have a charm unparalleled by the other books of Scripture. When there is illness in the family, one recites the psalms. In grief, the psalms are a source of solace. Much of the daily prayer service is comprised of the psalms.

> A man who had been childless came to the Steipler Gaon for a *berachah*, and when he and his wife were blessed with a child that year, he spread the word that it was the Gaon's blessing that had brought him a child.
>
> One day, HaGaon Rav Menachem Mann Shach visited the Steipler Gaon and referred to this incident. "I did not know that you were a performer of miracles," he said.
>
> The Steipler Gaon said, "I'll tell you what happened. This man came to me for a *berachah*, which I gladly gave him. But he said that he was not satisfied with a *berachah*, and that he wanted a promise, a guarantee that he would have a child. I told him that this was an absurd request, but he would not take 'No' for an answer. He kept on nagging me, and I could not get rid of him. I wanted to get back to my Talmud study, so I said, 'All right, I give you a promise,' and he went away.
>
> "After he left, I thought, *What did I do? How could I promise him a child?* So I began saying *Tehillim*, praying that he have a child."
>
> Rav Shach said, "Oh, so you said *Tehillim* for him? Then it's not a miracle!"

Having one's prayers answered through sincere reading of the psalms is a natural phenomenon, not a miracle.

David — the Sweet Minstrel of Israel

HAPPINESS

Some people think of *Koheles* (*Ecclesiastes*) as depressing. The opening phrase, "Vanity of vanities, all is vanity" (or more simply put, "Futility of futilities, all is futile"), certainly conveys a depressive attitude.

Everyone in the world strives for happiness, but there are as many definitions of happiness as there are people in the world! I addressed this topic in *Simchah — It's Not Just Happiness*, and I will not duplicate that material here.

Sometimes a concept is best defined by comparing it to its opposite, just as light can be best understood as the opposite of darkness.

I came across a definition of "unhappiness" that may shed some light on happiness. "Unhappiness is in not knowing what we want and killing ourselves to get it." This appears to describe *Koheles* fairly well.

If we observe much of humanity, our neighbors and yes, even ourselves, we may see a frenetic expenditure of energy. Yet few people have a well-defined goal. They are killing themselves to get something, but it is not at all clear what it is that they seek. As King Solomon writes, he pursued many goals, thinking they would bring him happiness, but was repeatedly disillusioned.

One beauty of *Mesillas Yesharim* (*Path of the Just*) by R' Moshe Chaim Luzzato (Ramchal) is that it opens with the chapter "What Is Man's Obligation in His World?" Even if one were to disagree with Ramchal's formulation of what that obligation is, the very fact that one has a concept of an obligation and a goal is a major step in the right direction.

People would not like to think of themselves as addicts, yet there is a similarity between the addict who sees the next drink or drug as satisfying him, and the person who strives to get something that he thinks will satisfy him. Both are disappointed to find that getting the object of their desire does not provide more than very brief satisfaction, and one is off on the chase for something else.

The fact is that when one has a goal, when one *really* knows what one wants in life, one can proceed methodically to get it, and one does not have to kill oneself chasing an ever-retreating fantasy.

THE DIVINE GIFT

The *Bnei Yisasschar* provides an interesting insight into the hero of Chanukah, the *Kohen Gadol*, Matisyahu (Mattathias). He says that the name can be divided into *mattas*, which means "gift," followed by three letters that spell G-d's Name. Mattisyahu can, therefore, be understood to mean "a gift from Hashem."

During the miracle of Purim, the Jews assembled, fasted, and prayed for Divine salvation. In contrast, under the Syrian yoke, they were forbidden to assemble and pray, and they could not join in communal prayer to elicit Divine help. Nevertheless, because Hashem knew that if they were victorious they would restore the Temple service, their *future* merit earned them Divine salvation. That is why the *Al HaNissim* paragraph inserted on Chanukah into the *Amidah,* which begins, "In the days of Mattisyahu," concludes with, "And *thereafter* Your children came and kindled lights in the Courtyard of Your Sanctuary." Although they could not elicit Divine salvation with prayer, it was given to them as a gift, because of the mitzvah they would do *thereafter*.

Psalm 121 is often recited on Chanukah; it begins, "Whence will come my salvation? My salvation shall come from Hashem, Creator of heaven and earth." The word for "my salvation" is *ezri*. The *Bnei Yisasschar* says there is a difference between two words that both mean salvation. *Ezer* is a salvation that is given without our asking for it, but Divine beneficence may be given when we have done something to merit it. Then it is called *yeshuah*, referred to as "elicited from below," i.e., by virtue of our good deeds. It may also be given as a Divine gift, "elicited from above," even though we may not have done anything to merit it (*ezer*). We may receive the Divine beneficence by virtue of our future merits.

When Hashem told Moses to deliver the Israelites from their enslavement in Egypt, Moses said, "Who am I that I should go to Pharaoh and that I should take the Children of Israel out of Egypt?" Hashem's answer was, "When you will take the people out of Egypt, you will serve Hashem on this mountain" (*Exodus* 3:11-12), Rashi says that Moses asked, "What merits do the Israelites have that they should be liberated?" Hashem's response was, "They have the merit that they will receive the Torah on this mountain," i.e., they have the merit of what they will do *in the future*.

The creation of the universe could not have been "elicited from below," because there was nothing in existence. Hashem created the universe by merit of the mitzvos that *tzaddikim* would do *in the future*. This is why Psalm 121 is recited on Chanukah. "Whence shall come my salvation (*ezri*)? My salvation (*ezri*) shall come from Hashem, Creator of heaven and earth." I.e., just as the creation of the world was not caused by anything that *had been* merited but by virtue of what would come about in the future, so the salvation of Chanukah was *ezer*, by virtue of future merits.

AN AVEIRAH, NOT A MITZVAH!

With regard to the mitzvah to drink on Purim, Rama says that one need not get drunk, but to drink just a bit more than one usually does, and then take a nap. The *Mishnah Berurah* (695) notes, "This is the proper thing to do." This is the halachah we must live by today. Getting drunk is *improper.* That is the halachah.

Experience in the past several years has been that young people particularly, who drink to excess on Purim, indulge in both shameful and dangerous behavior. Hatzolah cannot keep up with the calls to take these young men to hospital emergency rooms! Can anyone conceive that this is a mitzvah?

Beis Yosef quotes *Orchos Chaim:* "The mitzvah to drink on Purim does *not* mean to get drunk, because being drunk is a total *issur, and there is no aveirah greater than this!*" I believe that based on this, and the observation of the tragedies resulting from excess drinking on Purim, HaGaon HaRav Shmuel Kamenetzky made the bold statement, "Getting drunk on Purim is an *aveirah*, not a *mitzvah*."

Parents! Exercise your authority to prevent your children from harming themselves or others! Make it abundantly clear to them that you will not tolerate excessive drinking, regardless of what their misguided friends may do.

Baalei batim and Rebbeim! When *bachurim* visit your homes on Purim, do *not* serve them alcohol: neither wine, beer, nor liquor. They can have the permissible amount (no more than 4½ ounces of wine) at home, under their parents' supervision.

Remember this! If you serve a young man alcohol, and it has a harmful consequence to him or others, *you are responsible for any harm done!*

Rabbanim and Rebbeim! *Baruch Hashem*, our children look up to you for guidance. Help them and the community to stay healthy and well by speaking out unequivocally against getting drunk on Purim. They will listen to you more than to others.

May we all enjoy a truly joyous and safe Purim!

AUTHENTIC TORAH VALUES

One of the most poignant lectures I've ever given was presented to a group of parents of "special-needs children," children who were mentally and/or physically challenged to varying degrees. I began by telling the audience that I felt I was in the presence of the most authentic Torah-observant Jews. I have indeed been in some very *frum* gatherings and in various yeshivos, but none compared to this group.

Children who are mentally challenged may be very limited in their educability, and those with severe physical defects may not be able to perform many activities. Yet, according to Torah standards, they are not less worthy than people who are very learned and productive.

Torah law states that if a person is ordered to kill someone or else he will be killed, he must accept martyrdom and may not kill the other person. The Talmud's statement is, "What makes you think that your blood is redder? Perhaps the other person's blood is redder." In other words, you have no right to think that your life is more valuable than the other person's (*Pesachim* 25b).

Let's consider this scenario. The person who is being ordered to kill another is a very learned person who is a great teacher. He is also a philanthropist who helps many people. He is a pillar of the community. He is ordered to kill a person who is a renegade, a blight on society. There is no question in anyone's mind who is more worthy. According to Torah law, the scholar must allow himself to be killed because "What makes you think that your blood is redder? Perhaps the other person's blood is redder." Torah law does not operate according to society's standards. Every *neshamah* is of equal value.

Practically speaking, this Torah standard is often ignored. We live in a society that values productivity. A person's value is generally gauged by what he/she contributes to the community. We have been influenced by society's standards and we do apply them. Some educational institutions will accept only students who have the potential to excel. People of means are accorded higher honors and more privileges than those of lesser means. Special-needs children are viewed as being unproductive; this perception deprives them of value in the eyes of society.

The parents of a special-needs child who invest all their energy in bringing out all the potential in that child, even though he or she may not become a scholar nor accomplish a great deal, are practicing authentic Torah values. The sincere, simple prayer of a mentally challenged person is as meritorious as the prayer of a scholar who can meditate on the most intricate esoteric concepts.

In the ritual upon completing a volume of the Talmud, we say, "Torah scholars toil and receive reward, while they toil and do not receive reward." The Chofetz Chaim asked, "Are other workers not rewarded for their work? Isn't a tailor paid for his work?" He answered, "A tailor is paid for his work only when it leads to the making of a garment. If a tailor would put stitches into a piece of cloth that would never become a finished product, he would not be paid. Torah scholars are rewarded for their work of learning Torah even if it never leads to a finished product. There are portions of Talmud that will never be put to use, but one is still rewarded for learning them (*Sanhedrin* 71a).

> A Midrash states that a wise man came across several bewildered people standing near a well. They told him that they were servants, and that their master had sent them out to draw water from the well, but there were holes in the pitchers he had provided, so that the water ran out. The wise man said, "Your master knows there are holes in the pitchers, and if he wants you to draw water with them, then that's what you should do. He did not tell you to return with water. So you just do the drawing, and let the water run out."

We may not necessarily see the product resulting from our performance of mitzvos. Only Hashem knows what that product is. We must do the mitzvos even if we do not see a tangible product. This is the antithesis of society's values.

Parents do much for their children, but they look forward to the *nachas* they will reap from them. Some severely limited special-needs children may never be able to provide the anticipated *nachas* to their parents, yet the parents nurture this precious *neshamah,* expecting no return. That is authentic Torah value.

One mother of a special-needs child said, "When I realize how much I love this child even with his many shortcomings, that is when I can understand how Hashem can love me with all my shortcomings."

Taking care of a special-needs child can be a model for *avodas Hashem* (service of G-d). The basis of *Yiddishkeit* is in the declaration of *Shema Yisrael,* followed by *Ve'ahavta,* which means we are to serve Hashem with love, accepting the *yoke* of subjugating ourselves to the will of Hashem. The two concepts do not conflict. We may regard the service of Hashem as a yoke, yet we can accept it with love.

Parents of a special-needs child may indeed feel that providing all the care that the child needs, both physical and emotional, is a yoke, yet they accept this yoke with much love.

Yes, this group of parents was practicing authentic Torah values.

THERE'S ENOUGH BLAME TO GO AROUND

It is extremely common to look for someone or something to blame when anything goes wrong, and it is rather easy to find someone or something to blame. One who truly cannot find whom or what to blame tends to blame Hashem, because He is always there and is in charge of everything.

The propensity to blame is very deep seated and can overwhelm logic. The Torah relates that Jacob's wife, Rachel, was childless, while her sister Leah, Jacob's first wife, had many children. In exasperation, Rachel said to Jacob, "Give me children — otherwise I am dead!" (*Genesis* 30:1). When Rachel was ultimately blessed with a child, she said, "God has taken away my disgrace" (ibid. 30:23). To what disgrace was she referring? The Midrash says that Rachel said, "Now, if anything goes wrong, I can blame the child. If Jacob says, 'Who broke the dish?' or 'Who ate all the figs?' I can say, 'Your son did it'" (*Genesis 30:23, Rashi*).

I sincerely doubt that Rachel, who so longed for a child, harbored so inane a thought. Rather, this is the Torah's way of telling us how powerful the tendency to blame is. It is a profound psychological insight, and alerts us to be on our guard. It is easy to blame, but blaming is counterproductive.

The Torah relates that the first sin of humankind was eating the forbidden fruit of the Tree of Knowledge. Hashem chastised Adam, who put the blame on Eve. Eve, in turn, blamed the serpent. No one accepted blame. Perhaps if Adam and Eve had said, "Yes, we did it, and it was a mistake," they would have been forgiven. As long as a person blames others for the wrongs he or she does, there can be no forgiveness.

The reason for the widespread propensity to blame is simple. *If I can find someone or something to blame for my difficulties, I am absolved from the obligation to make any changes in myself.* The prototype of this is the alcoholic who blames his wife for his drinking. The message is, *Get her to change and I'll be fine. I don't have to make any effort at changing myself.* Few people are prepared to change themselves. We are creatures of habit, and if not frankly indolent, we all share the characteristic of everything else in nature: *inertia*. It takes effort to change the status quo, and unless we have no choice, we tend to resist exerting effort.

One place where this may cause problems is in psychotherapy. There is no doubt that early life experiences can have long-lasting effects. Moods and behavioral symptoms may indeed be traced back to things parents said and did during one's childhood. But the question is, "So what!?" The theory that understanding the sources of the symptoms will alleviate them, logical as it may sound, is not always proven in fact. It is not unusual for a patient to say, "I understand everything you said. I just don't feel any different."

On the other hand, when a symptom is ascribed to what parents said and/or did, it is not unusual for the patient to turn against the parent. When this happens, the patient may lose a relationship with someone whose love for him/her is deeper than that of anyone else in the world.

Bear in mind that one would not want someone else to take the credit and subsequent reward for something exceptional that he did. In the same vein, one must be prepared to face the consequences when he does something reprehensible.

As difficult as it is, we can never make changes for the better unless and until we are prepared to accept sole responsibility for our actions.

DESCARTES AND R' YERUCHEM

The philosopher Descartes is renowned for his dictum, "*Cogito ergo sum* — I think, therefore I am." Inasmuch as there is a phenomenon of hallucination, in which a person sees or hears things that do not exist, yet he is absolutely certain of their existence, Descartes raises the possibility, remote as it may be, that perhaps I am hallucinating. Nothing in the world exists, nothing that I see, hear, touch, taste, or smell. I may be hallucinating all these things. My body may be a hallucination. Perhaps I don't have arms or legs, and when I pinch myself to make sure I'm awake, that too may be hallucinatory. However, one thing is undeniable. Even if I am hallucinating everything, I must exist in order to be hallucinating. Perhaps I don't exist as a body, because that may be a hallucination. However, in some shape or form, I must exist; otherwise I could not be hallucinating. Hence, *cogito ergo sum* — I think, therefore I am.

Alongside hallucination as an error of reality testing, stands "delusion." Delusion is a fixed belief from which a person cannot be swerved by logical argument.

> A man who had the delusion that he was dead was brought to a psychiatrist. The psychiatrist asked him, "Do dead people bleed?"
>
> The man replied, "Of course not." The psychiatrist then had him recite 100 times, "Dead people do not bleed."
>
> He then pricked the man's finger, causing it to bleed. The man said, "Dead people *do* bleed."

R' Yeruchem Levovitz of Yeshivas Mir (*Daas Chochmah U'Mussar*, Vol. 2, pp. 139-142) cites the Talmudic statement that Job claimed, "The world was turned over to Satan" (*Job* 9:24), and states that this was indeed so. Satan was given the extraordinary power to delude people and even to cause them to hallucinate.

When Moses did not return from Sinai at the expected time, Satan told the Israelites that without food and water, Moses had perished, and he caused them to have a vision of Moses being carried on a bier (*Shabbos* 89a). With their own eyes, they saw that Moses had died!

The Torah says that a false prophet may arise who will claim that G-d has commanded us to worship an idol, and to prove his authenticity, the prophet will perform miracles. The Torah cautions us to beware of this charlatan, because this is Hashem's way of testing our loyalty to him. R' Yeruchem states that the ability to perform miracles to justify idolatry is an example of the power to delude that was given to Satan.

R' Yeruchem says that we live in a world of delusion. Moses warned us against thinking that our success is due to our own prowess. "You may say in your heart, 'My strength and the might of my hand made me all this wealth'" (*Deuteronomy* 8:17). Yet we think that if we spend ten hours a day at work, we will earn more than if we spent four hours a day at work, as if the time we invest in work determines how much we will earn. Everyone thinks this way, but it is a delusion.

Satan has caused us to think that our success depends on our effort.

> In Yellowstone National Park the geyser, Old Faithful, erupts regularly. Two pranksters brought a steering wheel and shaft, and placed themselves where they could be seen by tourists. The guide was in the process of regaling tourists with information about the precisely timed eruptions of Old Faithful, and just as the geyser was due to erupt, one prankster shouted to the other, "O.K.! Let 'er go!" The other prankster gave the wheel a sharp twist, and then the geyser erupted. Observers could believe that the eruption was produced mechanically.

So it is with us. Torah teaches us that, with the exception of choosing good or evil, which Hashem has left to the individual, Hashem controls *everything*, from the minutest to the most cataclysmic events. However, the way we live our lives seems to conflict with this belief. Rather, we act as if there is much that we can control. This, R' Yeruchem says, is the work of Satan, who causes us to be deluded.

So Descartes tells us that we may all be hallucinating, while R' Yeruchem says that we all live one massive delusion. Whereas we need not live our lives according to Descartes' philosophy, R' Yeruchem says that we must free ourselves of Satan's delusion. The only true reality is what Torah says is true. Everything else is delusional.

Ramchal in *Mesillas Yesharim* says that we were placed in a world replete with *nisyonos* (trials and tests). R' Yeruchem says that accepting what Torah says as the true reality and resisting the Satanic delusion is the *nisayon* with which we are all tested.

DECLARATION OF INDEPENDENCE VS. MESILLAS YESHARIM

In several Passover Haggados, the question is posed, "When the child asks the Four Questions about the Seder ritual, the father responds, 'We were slaves unto Pharaoh.' How does that answer the child's questions?" One explanation is that the father is saying, "When we were slaves to Pharaoh, we did not question his orders. We did what we were ordered to do. Hashem delivered us from Egypt and He is now our Master, We don't question his orders. We do as we are told."

At the Kosel, one frequently sees young men who urge visitors to put on *tefillin*. One young man was about to approach a man when his comrades said, "Don't bother. We've tried with him, but he just refuses. He is not religious and just visits the Kosel as a national shrine." Nevertheless, the young man approached the visitor.

"Pardon me," he said, "but aren't you General X?"

The man confirmed that he was.

The young man said, "I was in your battalion in the Golan. When you ordered us to take the hill, we thought it was suicide. But you were the general and we obeyed your orders. Here, there is another General, and we must obey His orders, whether we like to or not." Without a word, the general rolled up his sleeve and put on *tefillin*.

Whether it is a general and soldiers, or a king and his subjects, the master's orders must be obeyed.

Yes, we are Hashem's children (*Deuteronomy* 14:1), and we should relate to Him with the love and reverence of a child to a father, but that does not preclude our role as slaves. The knowledge that we are Hashem's children enables us to realize that whereas a human master assigns duties to his slaves for his own benefit, a devoted father has the child's best interest at heart, and the duties Hashem wishes us to carry out are for *our own benefit*, not for His.

In the Ten Commandments, Hashem made it very clear. "I am your G-d Who delivered you from the land of Egypt, from the house of enslavement." Subsequently, Hashem said, "For the Children of Israel are slaves to Me, whom I have taken out from the land of Egypt" (*Leviticus* 25:55). The only difference is that in Egypt we had no choice whether we wished to be Pharaoh's slaves or not, whereas with Hashem, we voluntarily accept our servitude to Him every day when we say the *Shema*. The Talmud tells us that by saying the *Shema* we subjugate ourselves to the "yoke of the Divine rule."

The Declaration of Independence states that among the "inalienable rights of man are life, liberty, and the pursuit of happiness." This is indeed a lofty concept. However, slaves do not have inalienable rights. Slaves are obligated to follow the master's orders. Slaves have only duties. *Slaves do not have rights.* We *do* pursue happiness, but we do so because it is a mitzvah, *v'hayisa ach samei'ach*

(*Deuteronomy* 16:15). Failure to serve Hashem with joy is a serious dereliction.

As stated above, Ramchal begins his epochal *Mesillas Yesharim* with "The obligation of a person in his world." This sets the theme for the entire treatise. If a person has inalienable rights, then he is free, within accepted limits, to decide how he wishes to exercise these rights. If one is a slave and has obligations and duties imposed upon him by a Master, then it is incumbent upon him to know how the Master wishes these duties to be carried out. This is further emphasized in the Talmud. "Nullify your will before Hashem's will" (*Ethics of the Fathers* 2:4).

A master wishes that his slaves be well nourished and healthy in order to be in optimum condition to perform their required duties. They should be well rested, because if fatigued, they cannot get the job done. If we see ourselves as slaves of Hashem, then everything we do should be in the interest of carrying out our obligations. We eat, sleep, recreate, work, and transact because these are essential to our fulfilling our obligations. "Nullify your will before Hashem's will" leaves no room for pursuits that are not directed to the service of Hashem.

Ramchal would fully agree with "life, liberty, and the pursuit of happiness." Life, because the Torah says, "You shall observe My decrees and My laws which man shall carry out and by which *he shall live*" (*Leviticus* 18:5). Liberty, because the Torah says, "Proclaim *freedom* throughout the land for *all its inhabitants*" (ibid. 25:10). Pursuit of happiness, because the Torah says, "You shall be *completely joyous*" (*Deuteronomy* 16:15). These are *inalienable* mitzvos, not merely rights!

DISCOVERING THE NUCLEUS OF BEAUTY

Hashem said to Abraham, "Gaze, now, toward the Heavens and count the stars .... So shall your offspring be" (*Genesis* 15:5).

A number of years ago, in Israel, I initiated a rehabilitation program for ex-convicts who had been imprisoned for drug-related crimes. In a session with the first group of clients, I pointed out that there is a natural resistance to avoid damaging an object of beauty. Inasmuch as everyone knows that drugs are damaging, there should have been greater resistance to their taking drugs. The reason they did not have this resistance was because they had never considered themselves to be worthy and beautiful. I said that long-term recovery depends on developing self-esteem, so that one would not want to damage himself.

One of the ex-convicts said, "How can you expect me to have self-esteem? I'm 34 years old, and 16 of those 34 years have been spent in prison. When I get out of prison, no one will give me a job. When the social worker tells my family that I will be released in 90 days, they are very unhappy. I am a burden and an embarrassment to them. They wish I would stay in jail forever — or even die. How am I supposed to develop self-esteem?"

I said to him, "Avi, have you ever seen a display of diamonds in a jewelry-store window? Those diamonds are scintillatingly beautiful and worth tens of thousands of dollars. Do you know what they looked like when they were brought out of the diamond mine? They looked like ugly, dirty pieces of glass, which anyone would think worthless.

"At the diamond mine, there is a *mayvin* [expert] who scrutinizes the ore. He may pick up a 'dirty piece of glass' and marvel at the precious gem that lies within. He sends it to the processing plant, and it emerges as a magnificently beautiful, shining diamond.

"No one can put any beauty into a dirty piece of glass. The beauty of the diamond was always there, but it was concealed by layers of material that covered it. The processing plant removed these layers, to bring to light the beauty of the diamond. They did not *create* the beauty, just revealed it.

"I may not be a *mayvin* on diamonds, Avi," I concluded, "but I am a *mayvin* on people. You have a beautiful *neshamah* within you, but it has been covered with layers of ugly behavior. We will help you get rid of those layers and reveal the beauty of your *neshamah*."

Avi stayed in the program for several months and then moved to a transitional facility for eight months. After leaving, he found a job and remained free of drugs.

One day, Annette, the administrator of the program, received a call from a family whose elderly mother had died, leaving an apartment full of furniture for which they had no use. They offered to donate the furniture to the rehabilitation program. Annette called Avi and said, "I have no way of getting that furniture here. Could you help us?" Avi assured her that he would get a truck and bring the furniture.

Discovering the Nucleus of Beauty

Two days later, Avi called Annette. "I am at the apartment," he said, "but there is no point in bringing the furniture. It is old and dilapidated."

Annette said, "I don't want to disappoint the family, Avi. Bring it here. Perhaps we can salvage some of it."

Avi loaded the truck and brought the furniture to the facility, which was on the second floor of the building. As he dragged an old sofa up the stairs, an envelope fell from the cushions. It contained 5000 shekels ($1800 US). This was money of whose existence no one was aware, and the rule of "finders-keepers" could easily have been applied, especially by someone who used to break into a house for ten shekels.

Avi called Annette and told her about the money. "That's the family's money," she said. "Call them and tell them." The family graciously donated the money to the rehabilitation program.

On a subsequent visit to Israel, I met Avi at a function of the rehabilitation program, and that is when Annette told me the story about the 5000 shekels.

I said to Avi, "Do you remember our first meeting when you did not know how you could ever have self-esteem? I told you that there was a soul, a beautiful diamond within you. Many people who never stole a penny would have simply pocketed the money. What you did was truly exceptional, and shows the beauty of the 'diamond' within you."

Several months later, Avi affixed a bronze plaque on the door of the rehabilitation center. It read *"DIAMOND PROCESSING CENTER."*

Abraham's offspring are indeed like the stars.

KEVOD HABERIOS (HUMAN DIGNITY)

The Torah ascribes the greatest importance to human dignity. *Gadol kevod haberios* — the dignity of a person is so great that it sometimes overrides rabbinic ordinances (*Berachos* 19b). Although one's sins do not cancel one's mitzvos — one is rewarded for mitzvos and punished for sins — if one humiliates a person publicly, one forfeits his portion in the World to Come (*Ethics of the Fathers* 3:15).

There is an amazing Midrash in *Eichah Rabbah* (Introduction to Item 24). At the time of the destruction of Jerusalem and the brutal murder of the Israelites, the patriarch Abraham came before Hashem. "All my life I hoped to have a child, and at age 100 You gave me a child. Years later, You told me to bring him as an offering. I did not question You nor did I hesitate. I hurried to fulfill Your command. Is this my reward: to see my children banished and tortured?" Hashem did not respond nor even acknowledge Abraham.

The patriarch Isaac came before Hashem. "I was 37 years old when my father brought me as an offering. I could have resisted. Yet, I complied and asked my father to bind me tightly to the altar, lest I inadvertently resist. I willingly gave up my life for You. Is this my reward?" Hashem did not respond nor even acknowledge Isaac.

The patriarch Jacob came before Hashem. "I totally devoted myself to Torah study. I was persecuted by Esau and Laban, but I endured all the suffering in order to father the Twelve Tribes that You wanted, and now the children I sought to bring into the world are being killed. Is this my reward?" Hashem did not respond nor even acknowledge Jacob.

Moshe Rabbeinu came before Hashem. "You thrust the care of the children of Israel on me. For 40 years I carried them on my back like the burden on a horse. I sustained great suffering from them, but tolerated it all to fulfill Your wish. Is this my reward, to see the people I cared for destroyed?" Hashem did not respond nor even acknowledge *Moshe Rabbeinu*.

Then the matriarch Rachel came before Hashem. "You know how much Jacob loved me and how much I loved him. I knew my father was deceitful and that he would try to substitute my sister Leah in my place. I, therefore, gave Jacob a secret sign, whereby he could tell if it was me or Leah.

"When I saw my father taking Leah to the wedding, I realized that if Jacob made use of the secret sign, Leah would be humiliated. To prevent her being humiliated, I gave her the secret sign.

"I was ready to give up the man I loved to my sister, and deprive myself of the man I loved for my entire life. Is this my reward, to see my children destroyed?"

Hashem responded to Rachel. "It is by your merit, Rachel, that your children will be returned to their land."

Think of it! The pleas of the great patriarchs, Abraham, Isaac, and Jacob, are ignored. Their immense virtues are not acknowledged. The one virtue that will bring Jews salvation is that of Rachel, who was willing to sacrifice her entire future for what? To spare her sister *just a few moments of embarrassment*!

That is how important the dignity of a person is.

There are many occasions when we are put to the test. We relate with people who may offend or provoke us, and our first impulse is to react aggressively, possibly causing someone embarrassment. The above Midrash should make us cognizant of how cautious we must be not to impugn a person's dignity.

APPRECIATION

I received the following request for help.

> *I have been married for four years and have two adorable children. The problem is that my husband has never shown any appreciation to me and has never said a thank-you after I serve him his food. I feel that our shalom bayis is at risk because of all this. Please help.*

It is extremely irritating to feel that your efforts are not appreciated. I wish there were a way to change your husband's attitude, but such change is unlikely to happen unless he realizes that there is something wrong with his attitude. Perhaps I can suggest something that will help reduce your irritation and your anger at his "apparent" lack of appreciation. I say "apparent" because he may in fact appreciate what you do, but is unable to show it.

The Talmud says that Moses reprimanded the Israelites as being "ingrates, the sons of ingrates" (*Avodah Zarah* 5a). The first ingrate was Adam, who, instead of being grateful to Hashem for giving him his wife, said, "The woman You gave me made me eat it," thus putting the blame on Hashem (*Rashi, Genesis* 3:12).

In what way were the Israelites ingrates? When they were afraid to hear the voice of Hashem as He gave them the Ten Commandments and they asked Moses to intercede, Hashem said, "Who would assure that this heart should remain theirs to fear Me ... all the days" (*Deuteronomy* 5:26). Moses asked the Israelites, "Why did you not say to Hashem, 'You [Hashem] assure'?" Tosafos explain that they did not want to ask Hashem for assistance, thus demonstrating an unwillingness to be grateful to another — specifically, to Hashem

This is an important insight. A person may be reluctant to express appreciation or even *feel* appreciation because it makes him feel beholden, and this feeling is unpleasant.

I believe that ingratitude is rooted in low self-esteem. A person who feels inferior, even if the feeling is unwarranted by the truth, may feel that accepting a favor or being in any way dependent on someone else is a put-down. If your husband felt better about himself, it would be easy for him to say, "Thank you."

There is no way you can change your husband. That is up to him. However, this explanation may minimize your anger and irritation if you realize it is a result of his unwarranted feelings of inferiority. I discuss this concept in *Angels Don't Leave Footprints*. He does appreciate you, but just can't show it. It may be effective for you to model the proper behavior by thanking him for whatever he does for you and for his work and/or learning Torah. You can thereby increase his self-esteem and possibly help him to overcome his feelings of inferiority.

LIFE, LIBERTY, AND THE PURSUIT OF MISERY

I call heaven and earth today to bear witness against you: I have placed life and death before you, blessing and curse; and you shall choose life, so that you will live, you and your offspring (*Deuteronomy* 30:19).

With 50 years of psychiatric experience to my credit, I feel qualified to paraphrase the Founding Fathers' statement in the Declaration of Independence, that among the inalienable rights of man are "Life, liberty, and the pursuit of misery."

But what normal person would pursue misery instead of happiness? From the words of Moses, it is evident that it is necessary to tell people to choose life and blessing over death and curse. In fact, Moses also had to increase their motivation for this choice by telling them that the choice they make will have an impact on future generations. Clearly there are people who would choose death and curse, but why?

After having treated thousands of alcoholics and drug addicts, the answer became obvious. In active addiction, the person pursues the object of his addiction with a ferocity that is unparalleled. He will do anything to attain what he feels is the greatest blessing in life, although it is in fact the greatest curse. One recovered addict said, "The worst day of my recovery is far better than the best day of my addiction." However, the desire for the chemical blinds the addict to reality.

Whereas the lethality of chemicals is obvious to the non-addict, there are other desires that are no less lethal, but their toxicity is more subtle. The Talmud says, "Jealously, lust, and glory *remove a person from the world*" (*Ethics of the Fathers* 4:28). "Remove a person from the world" should be taken literally. These are insatiable drives, and unless a person puts firm limits and tight restraints on them, their pursuit may take one's life. Yet so many people pursue these drives, no less deluded than the addict in believing that they will bring happiness. Yes, there may be momentary pleasure in gratifying these drives, just as the addict has a fleeting "high" from his chemical, but the long-term result is anything but happy.

Recovery from the fatal pursuit of chemical addiction requires that the addict seek a spiritual goal in life, rather than the ephemeral "high." This is equally true for those who are deluded to think that pursuit of jealousy, lust, and glory will bring them happiness. Only true spirituality can turn them away from the pursuit of misery to the pursuit of happiness.

ROSH HASHANAH VS. NEW YEAR

On the night of December 31, many people gather to usher in the new year. Typically, alcohol is imbibed in huge quantities, and when the clock strikes midnight, the cry "Happy New Year!" is shouted by inebriated souls.

This is a rather strange phenomenon. Alcohol, when used in more than a *l'chaim* amount, is an emotional anesthetic, and is generally imbibed by individuals who are seeking relief from anxiety or other unpleasant feelings. People who feel happy would hardly wish to squelch a pleasant feeling. Can it be that these people are not as happy as they seem?

Generally, one day flows into the next and one week flows into the next. We rarely stop to take inventory of what is going on in our lives.

Certain events, however, may interrupt the routine of our lives and cause us to take a look at what we are accomplishing.

December 31 may be one such event. "What? It is already 2011? What happened to 2010? Why, I was just getting comfortable dating my checks '2010.' So, another year has passed. Another year of my life is behind me. And just what have I to show for it? Am I wealthier than before? No way! I'm deeper in debt than ever. Am I wiser than before? Hardly. Do I have reason to think that next year is going to be better? Not really."

These are depressing thoughts. One can hardly greet the new year cheerfully when the past year seems to have been largely wasted, and the next year doesn't look any more promising. The only way one can declare "Happy New Year" is to get drunk and forget about these depressing facts. New Year's Eve is one massive depression!

How different Rosh Hashanah is when properly observed! The preceding month of Elul was spent in *teshuvah* of increasing intensity, culminating in a week of *selichos,* special prayers for forgiveness. We review the events of the past year, identify mistakes we have made, and resolve to improve our character traits. We try to make amends to anyone we may have offended. We look forward to the forgiveness of Yom Kippur, when we will start with a clean slate. We can see why the next year will be better. With a well-functioning, sober mind, we wish each other *"L'shanah tovah tikaseivu,* May you be inscribed for a good year." Even the greeting is different. We wish *others* a good year, and in return, we are the recipients of their blessings.

We can be happy on Rosh Hashanah. Although Rosh Hashanah is indeed a solemn day on which we are judged, it is nevertheless a festival. After reprimanding the people for their sins on Rosh Hashanah, the prophet Nehemiah said, "Do not be sad. Eat and drink and send gifts to those who do not have, because the joy of G-d is your strength" (*Nehemiah* 8:10). Yes, we do celebrate the onset of the new year, but we do so with the dignity that befits a human being

KEEPING SECRETS

The issue of secrecy about medical and/or psychiatric conditions is very sensitive and painful. There are understandable reasons for concealing things, but there may be serious consequences of concealment. The question comes up in a broad range of situations.

> One woman who suffered from cancer did not want her children, ages 10 – 14, to know of it. She underwent chemotherapy, which resulted in a few disabling days. She thought the children were not aware of it, but somehow they found out she was receiving chemotherapy. However, because the dreaded word "cancer" was never used, the children felt that it must be so horrible a condition that it could not even be mentioned. They did not want to let on that they knew. Everybody was walking around in a daze, trying to keep secrets from one another. Instead of being able to support one another, they were living in tension, walking on eggshells.

After the woman passed away, one daughter who was particularly close with her was depressed because she had not been able to properly share many feelings with her mother and because she wondered if her mother had bottled up her own emotions in an attempt to spare her children.

Of course, a major consideration in our community is *shidduchim*, and if it is known that there is any kind of illness in a family, a red flag is raised. A professor of genetics who addresses these problems says, "If you do not want your child to marry into a family where there is a genetic disease, you might as well resign yourself to your child never getting married. There is no such thing as a family without some form of genetic condition!" However, people still shy away from a family where it is known there is some kind of illness, and logic may not change their minds.

Certainly when a *shidduch* is in progress, the question of revealing an existing condition comes up. In those instances where a *significant* condition was not revealed and came to light after the marriage, the results are invariably disastrous, and may cause repercussions affecting other members of the family. There is a loss of trust and a feeling of having been deceived that may never heal.

In addition, there are halachic guidelines. The Chofetz Chaim says that if someone knows about a condition that the prospective *chasan* or *kallah* had, and that if the other side knew of it they might not agree to the *shidduch*, one is obligated to reveal it because of *lo saamod al dam rei'acha* (do not stand by the blood of your neighbor; i.e., do not ignore your neighbor's suffering) (*Leviticus* 19:16).

What constitutes a "significant" condition? Insofar as marriage is concerned, any condition that may recur and that may affect the relationship is significant. People may ask a Rav for advice. If the Rav has *thorough* knowledge of the condition, he may give advice. If he does not have such knowledge, he should refrain from giving advice, and refer the question to someone who does have the requisite expertise, or consult with an expert in the field before responding.

People may have misconceptions about many conditions, and

may make important decisions based on erroneous information. One should avail himself of authoritative information about any condition.

> In one case, a young man was functioning normally, but was taking medication for a psychiatric condition. On the fifth date, he told the young woman about it, gave her the name and number of his doctor, and suggested she call to get the facts. She was satisfied that he can live a normal life and the *shidduch* was completed.

Perhaps the most important thing to realize is that there is really no way to ensure total concealment. You may think you are keeping the condition a secret, but the fact is that these attempts invariably fail, and the truth is discovered one way or another.

Secrets isolate. Man was not created to live an isolated existence, and we can gain strength from the support of other people. It would be foolish to make a public declaration of a condition, but the other extreme, keeping it a tight secret, may be just as unwise. Our own judgment about what we should reveal and what we should conceal may be influenced by our emotions. We should seek competent *daas Torah* advice on such issues.

SHALOM BAYIS AND WHO AM I

My book *Without a Job, Who Am I?* addresses the problem that arises when one's identity is totally dependent on one's job, on what one *does* rather than on who one *is*. This has far-reaching implications on *shalom bayis*.

Shalom bayis can be simply described as being comprised of two ingredients: mutual love and respect. The Talmud states this succinctly: "A husband should love his wife as he loves himself, and should respect her even more than he respects himself" (*Yevamos* 62b). Of course, this also holds true for the wife's attitude toward the husband.

It is of interest that in citing this Talmudic statement, Rambam reverses the order, placing respect before love. I believe this is because it is unrealistic to expect intense love to occur on Day One. Such love needs time to develop. However, respect should begin from the very first moment of the relationship.

Providing sustenance for one's family is, of course, essential. However, it is not enough to earn respect. Although having a job and earning a livelihood is of the utmost importance, it does not define one as a true human being. Rather, one is then merely *Homo sapiens*.

When a husband and wife each work on development of *middos*, subjecting their animal nature to the rule of the spiritual, they earn each other's respect. They are then able to look beyond their own needs in consideration of the needs of the spouse. This fulfills the Talmudic criterion for a happy marriage: to love one's wife as he loves himself, and respect her even more than he respects himself, and, of course, the reciprocal attitude of the wife toward the husband.

I venture to say that when there is lack of mutual respect in a marriage, it is little more than a peaceful coexistence, which is a fragile relationship. One should not be deluded that providing an income, even a handsome income, is enough to earn respect. Respect is gained when a person makes the effort to rise above the state of *Homo sapiens*, and fulfill oneself as a true human being, a real *mentsch*.

Husbands and wives should be introspective and say to themselves, *What am I doing to be respected by my spouse?*

CLEAVING TO HASHEM

Sixty-five years ago, in high school, I learned a powerful *mussar* lesson, but I did not realize it at the time.

Ulysses was a mythical hero and traveler. He heard of the "music of the sirens." This was music that was heard at a particular narrow passage between reefs, and it was so enchanting, so alluring, that it drew sailors to the shore, where their ships were smashed on the rocks. Sailors knew this, and, when passing the reefs from a distance, they would see the wreckage of the ships that had been destroyed. Nevertheless, as they drew near the strait and heard the music of the sirens, they were helpless and headed to their own destruction.

Ulysses wanted to hear the fabled music of the sirens, but knew that it would be fatal. He, therefore, filled his sailors' ears with wax so that they could not hear any sounds, and he told them that they were to sail by the danger zone and pay no attention to anything he said. He then had himself lashed securely to the ship's mast so that he could not move.

As the ship approached the rocks, Ulysses began to hear the music of the sirens. He began shouting to the sailors to head for shore, but of course, they could not hear him. He began screaming at them, "I am your captain! You must obey my orders!" As he heard the music of the sirens, he struggled to free himself from the ropes. "Head for the shore!" he shouted. "I will have you hanged for mutiny!" But the sailors rowed on.

After they had safely passed through the channel and the music was no longer heard, Ulysses fainted from exhaustion. The sailors then untied him, and he realized how helpless he had been in the grip of the music; had he not rendered the sailors unable to hear, they would have all been destroyed.

Much later I realized that the "music of the sirens" is the *yetzer hara*. It can enchant a person and render him almost helpless to resist its temptation. Seeing the wreckage of the ships that had attempted the passage did not prevent sailors from rowing to their destruction.

A drug addict worked in a mortuary and prepared for burial the corpses of people who had died from drug usage, but that did not stop his use, and he, too, died from the results of his addiction at age 33. Drugs, music of the sirens, *yetzer hara* — they are all the same.

There is no way we can "close our ears" to the "music of the sirens" that can be heard almost anywhere in our environment. The Talmud cites Hashem as saying, "I created the *yetzer hara*, and I created Torah as its antidote" (*Kiddushin* 30b). It is our only defense. However, just holding on to Torah is not enough, just as Ulysses' holding on to the mast would not have been enough. We must tie ourselves so tightly to Torah that we can not break loose from it. This is why Moses repeatedly stresses, "But you who *cling* to Hashem — you are all alive today" (*Deuteronomy* 4:4), "to Him you shall *cleave*," (ibid. 10:20) and "To love Hashem, to listen to His voice and to *cleave* to Him (ibid. 30:20). King David says, "I have *clung* to Your testimonies (*Psalms* 119:31). To cling and cleave means to be inseparably attached to Torah.

Learning Torah and doing mitzvos is of greatest importance, but does not yet result in the necessary fusion. The Talmud says that the single verse that the entire Torah depends on is "Know Hashem in all your ways" (*Proverbs* 3:6; *Berachos* 63a). Cleaving and clinging are not accomplished by relating to Hashem merely in Torah study and in performance of mitzvos, but in everything we do: eating, sleeping, transacting, socializing. The works of *mussar* tell us how we can accomplish this. It is this kind of observance of Torah that can save us from the destructive attractions of the *yetzer hara*.

When you pick up a fruit, think of the meaning of the *berachah* "*borei pri ha'eitz*." Hashem designed a tree that would sprout from a tiny seed and produce succulent fruit — and you will feel gratitude to Hashem. When you say the *berachah* "*po'kei'ach ivrim*," think of the wondrous ability that Hashem instituted within protoplasm so that it can produce vision, and feel gratitude to Hashem. If we bring Hashem into all our activities, we are cleaving and clinging to Him, and when we tie ourselves securely to the mast, we can avoid the *yetzer hara's* "music of the sirens" that would draw us to our own destruction.

YIRAS CHEIT (FEAR OF SIN) – AHAVAS HASHEM (LOVE OF G-D)

As circumstances in the world change, we must adapt properly to preserve our lives. I remember when one could arrive at the airport a half-hour before flight time and board in a leisurely fashion. Today, because of the terrorist threat, we must be at the airport much earlier to pass security and have our baggage x-rayed. I remember when my dentist did not wear gloves and a mask when working on my teeth. Today, because of the danger of HIV and hepatitis, the dentist must take precautions.

Since the days of Adam and Eve, there was sin in the world, but the prevailing public concepts of morality and decency provided some safety. Today, with provocative billboards and magazine covers at the supermarket checkout, with flagrant lewdness on the Internet, with constitutional sanction of obscenity and vulgarity in the media, and with the erosion of judgment due to the widespread use of mind-altering drugs, our environment has become a cesspool of immorality. It is a major challenge to maintain one's morality and to raise children in such an environment.

Filters on the Internet and attempts to restrict access to objectionable material cannot stem the tide. The only effective method is to elevate ourselves to a level of spirituality so that our pride in being a true human being rather than a beast with intellect will prevent us from yielding to base desires. We have to understand sin as being debasing and recognize the dangers posed by our environment. Sincere study of Torah ethics in *Pirkei Avos* (*Ethics of the Fathers*) and the writings of *mussar* can make us aware of what we can be and what we should be. Implementing these principles in our daily lives can elevate us to a level of spirituality that will dignify us as human beings.

In the works of *mussar*, *yiras Hashem* (reverence of G-d) is always linked to *ahavas Hashem* (love of G-d). Many commentaries discuss the question, "How can one be commanded to love G-d?" Love is an emotion, and one cannot generate an emotion at will.

The Talmud actually provides an answer to this question, by translating *ve'ahavta es Hashem* not as, "You shall love G-d," but rather as "You shall make G-d beloved by others" (*Yoma* 86a). This, the Talmud says, is achieved by transacting honestly, speaking pleasantly, and behaving in a manner that will cause others to say, "How wonderful it is to observe the Torah! It makes people so refined." This type of *ahavas Hashem* is within everyone's capability.

Fulfilling *ahavas Hashem* by character refinement discourages us from yielding to our animalistic drives, and contributes substantially to *yiras cheit*.

In true Torah observance, how one relates vis-à-vis Hashem and vis-à-vis other people are inseparable. *Yirah* and *ahavah* indeed go together, and provide the only effective defense against sinking into the quicksand of immorality that threatens us and our children.

BE CAREFUL WHAT YOU PRAY FOR

There is a common adage, "Be careful what you pray for. You might get it."

This brings to mind a delightful tale.

In the village of Constantin lived a *tzaddik*, R' Daniel. His wife, a great *tzaddeikes*, was very upset one week when there was no fish in the market for Shabbos. Friday morning, she went to the market and saw that a huge fish was being delivered to a store. She promptly bought the fish and joyfully said, "Master of the universe! You have been so kind to me to provide me with a fish for Shabbos. Now, please provide me with a proper guest for Shabbos."

In the nearby village of Drobitsch, the *tzaddik*, R' Yitzchak, was suddenly overcome by an urge to go to Constantin for Shabbos. He could not explain this urge, but it was irresistible. When he told his wife that he was going to Constantin for Shabbos, she said, "But you never travel on Friday."

R' Yitzchak said, "I really have no choice."

He hired a horse and carriage, and headed to Constantin, not knowing where or why he was going.

The horse stopped at the home of R' Daniel, who welcomed R' Yitzchak heartily. They spent a Shabbos of great *kedushah*, studying Torah and particularly the hidden kabbalistic meanings. At the *shalosh seudos* (the third Shabbos meal), R' Yitzchak told R' Daniel how much he had enjoyed spending Shabbos with him, but he had no idea how this had come about.

R' Daniel's wife said, "I'm afraid it was my fault," and related how she had prayed to have a proper Shabbos guest.

R' Yitzchak said, "Your prayers are powerful. Henceforth you should be careful what you pray for."

Perhaps we protect ourselves from improper prayers when we say, in the blessing for the new month, that Hashem should bless us with "a life in which our heartfelt requests will be fulfilled *for the good.*" I.e., if we pray for something that will not be good for us, we waive that request.

TEFILLAH – OUR ONLY HOPE

In the 16th century, R' Chaim Vital, the leading disciple of the Arizal, wrote, "In our generation, with the moral pollution of the atmosphere, there is no defense against the *yetzer hara* except *tefillah b'kavannah* [meaningful prayer]" (cited in *Yesod VeShoresh HaAvodah*, 2:89). That was more than 400 years ago!

I can't imagine what kind of terrible pollution there could have been then. Why, I recall that in my childhood, only 70 years ago, there was no detrimental pollution of the atmosphere. Radio programs and the printed media were relatively decent. Even when television came on the scene, most programming consisted of clean comedy and sitcoms. Today, the frank obscenity in all the media, printed and graphic, is offensive to anyone with a sense of morality.

The smut on the Internet is readily accessible in the home, office, or "smart phone."

If *tefillah b'kavannah* was the only salvation from the *yetzer hara* 400 years ago, what can we say today? It seems that if we wish to save ourselves and our children from the wiles of the *yetzer hara*, we should be praying tearfully and reciting *Tehillim* (*Psalms*) many hours during the day!

We can learn something from medicine. Doctors are very concerned that many of the antibiotics that had been effective against infections have lost their potency because the bacteria have become resistant to them. Years ago, penicillin cured most infections, but today, penicillin may accomplish little. Scientists are in a frantic search for more potent antibiotics.

In the past, we kept the *yetzer hara* at bay by Torah study and by traditional *tefillah*. This may no longer be adequate. The *yetzer hara* is attacking us with unprecedentedly powerful weapons.

The number of youngsters who have fallen victim to drugs and other destructive behaviors is alarming. This is occurring even in Torah-observant families. The daily *davening*, meritorious as it is, is simply not enough to combat today's *yetzer hara*.

We should give serious attention to the words of R' Chaim Vital. Intense *tefillah b'kavannah*, both quantitative and qualitative, may be our only hope.